# THE TROPHY HUSBAND

## THE RAMBLINGS OF A PUB OWNER DURING A PANDEMIC

From the Creator of Dad Joke Genius and Co-owner of Shakespeare's Pub and the Universal Snack Patrol

Ted Vadella
ted@shakespearespub.com

For my family…

Without all of you, my life would be less amusing, uplifting, and fulfilled.

To my sons Alex and Rowan, I am forever grateful to be your father. You have made life worth living.

To my wife, Angela, who left me to my own devices, possibly against her better judgement. Sometimes saying "I love you" doesn't cover it all…

To my mother. My rock. You will forever be my protector and life guide. As you once said,

"My cup is so full" …

# THE TROPHY HUSBAND

## INTRODUCTION

March 16, 2020 was the first day of the Covid-19 restaurant lockdown. The eve of the biggest day, 16 years running, for Shakespeare's Pub, a place I have co-owned since its inception in 2003. The time, money, and preparation that goes into a St. Patrick's Day at Shakespeare's in Kalamazoo, MI is immeasurable. March 17$^{th}$ is our busiest day. The equivalent of the Super Bowl to our downtown watering hole. Doors open at 7am, and there is a line in a sea of green-wearing patrons waiting for live music, green beer, and Guinness. You can feel the energy, and its electric. For me, it's my favorite workday of the year. This year though? This year was anxiety-filled and uncertain. The drive in at 9am on March 16$^{th}$ didn't help to ease that. The announcement from the State Government coming in for restaurants to close at 3pm for the next 14 days. This was real, and we were living through something that hadn't been done in 100 years. A National pandemic. The uncertainty that we could recover from the investment into March 17$^{th}$ existed. It was only 14 days though, maybe we could just do a redo? Or maybe 14 days was wishful thinking.

## Shakespeare's Pub

For as long as I can remember, I have had a 40+ hour work week. When I was younger, it was mixed in with full-time school. Even younger than that, under the table jobs of fetching golf balls and cleaning racquetball and squash courts. I was always busy. I started dating my future wife, Angela, just before my partner, Scott and I, opened Shakespeare's Pub. Working as an investment consultant and Assistant Branch Manager at a bank, spending my spare time writing a business plan, and juggling that with having a 2-year-old son part time from a previous relationship that didn't work out. Looking at it now, my wife sacrificed so much to make us work. She understands me, and that I do this. My focus separates me, most certainly irritates people, and leaves little room for distractions. She left me to my own devices, and that is kind of the theme of our entire relationship. I love her for it, and I will never be able to say how much. 21 years and counting...

Scott and I opened Shakespeare's Pub on July 19th, 2003. We are the only owners of what has become a landmark pub for downtown Kalamazoo. The first time I heard an advertisement for a neighboring business, stating they were located across the street from Shakespeare's, I knew we made it. We have seen so much in the many years since 2003 that have helped us succeed. A Detroit Pistons NBA championship, a Detroit Red Wings NHL Stanley Cup, A USA Women's soccer team Gold Medal, and World Cup (twice), and even an 0-16 Detroit Lions team (Next year is our year! etc.). We tap 44 draft beers each July 19th that have never been tapped in the city of Kalamazoo before from breweries all around the country. We were the first to open our doors at 7am on March 17th. A move that was considered "silly" when we did it. It was busy that morning and had been every year, ever since.

I worked every day, in some fashion or another, whether it be at the pub or from my home. There is always something to do, and I am always "on". I don't really know how to shut it down and relax. My wife, Angela, (who I often refer to as "my wife" rather than her given name, because I am so proud, she is my wife.) has always been the vacation planner. If she didn't, I would never leave my own personal bubble of work and home. I never know I need a vacation until we get to the actual destination. More times than not, I tell her I would retire where she takes us. The multiple times we have gone to Wisconsin Dells, and I have looked at the possibility, or Hawaii, which is the ultimate goal. Both are polar opposites of each other really, but in the end, the most relaxed I have ever been are at destinations my wife has shown me.

Many times, Scott and I have had the discussion of our love for what we do. We built Shakespeare's together, over years of planning and hoping someone would take a chance on us to open our own place. Working in the bar industry was a college job that supplemented both of us getting through school, but the potential for it to be lucrative and us being young adults made us strive to succeed in a city with 3 colleges. This art deco building in the outskirts of a broken up downtown which was being revitalized seemed like a risky bet that maybe today, we wouldn't have made. Quite honestly, I wasn't sold on the location; an old fishing rod and reel company that closed its doors in the late 80's and sold its name to a Carolina sporting goods company. Shakespeare fishing rods was a centerpiece in Kalamazoo business and the history of the building, along with the front overhead etched in stone was the title, "Shakespeare Company", which still exists to this day. The windows were blown out, and the rear of the building was hollowed from a fire. Scott brought me to this very cold building during my lunch break on a February afternoon where I had a suit on, but no winter jacket. After 2 hours of listening to him ramble (Scott's a rambler) about how it was a great location vs. my hesitance, I asked, "If I say yes, can I go home?" He agreed. I went home and told my wife that I think I put us in certain bankruptcy.

People say it's hard having a partnership, and to those people I say, you don't have the right partner. Scott and I are brothers. Family. Although, we aren't related. He is the ultimate optimist at times and during others when he isn't I seem to fill in the void. We rarely disagree, and have similar values, and both of us work, and work, and work. A lot of our success was foresight, but just as much can be consider luck. We became a craft beer bar because at the time, no one else was doing that. Everyone had Budweiser and Miller products, and a Bell's beer because it was local, but any other microbrewery was a hard sell. Being a craft beer bar differentiated us from our competition, and I learned so much about beer from these artisan brewers that I attribute most of our success to their knowledge. I started doing Craft Beer events on Tuesdays where I would bring in a different brewery to send a representative to talk about their beer, and with our carry-out license, we did mix-or-match 6 packs to-go of all the styles from each brewery. All I wanted was a T-shirt, and what I got was an education of what these men and women do. It was easy to be the first in town to tap a beer that no one else had because at the time, no one else wanted them. After a while, I was buying a distributors entire inventory of small batch beers because they were new and shiny. We got a following from the craft beer community, and little by little, as craft beer started to ascend to great heights, we saw competition rise. By then, we had already established ourselves as a premiere craft beer bar in the city, and in the State of Michigan, and for a long time, we were the largest account for many different breweries.

We were the first to tap Short's Brewing Company beer in Kalamazoo, and they make a beer for us called "Ironic Ale" (based on my love for beer, even though I don't drink barely ever or more than samples at a time). Arbor Brewing's, "Euchre Pils" got its name from a phone call I made to Arbor's founders, Matt and Rene Greff, while sitting by a bonfire in my backyard and telling them that their Pilsner had a stupid name "Free Parking Pils" (Matt has always been receptive to my abrupt and insulting nature at times, which I owe him many apologies for) and that being from Michigan, people needed a beer for playing cards, and Euchre is a Michigan card game if ever there was one (You can look it up on their website, they still give me credit for the name in the description). Even Larry Bell himself changed his Octoberfest tap topper because I said it needed to be blue and white checkered like an Octoberfest is meant to be. It has made for great industry stories, and there are plenty I am sure that others would share that aren't as flattering, and to those stories, I am sorry for leaving a poor impression. It was never meant to be that way.

I haven't slept past 7am in years and hadn't been to bed before midnight since I was 16. An average night of sleep for me was between 4-5 hours. I have never been diagnosed with ADHD, but my wife will swear that I have it. I have "FOMO" (Fear Of Missing Out, I just learned this) and sleep gets in the way of that.

For the better part of the last 7 years though, my lack of sleep and early rising was due to a spoiled chihuahua (she's the worst) that we were given from a family member who could no longer care for her. We adopted Riley the chihuahua at 2 years of age, and if you have ever had a chihuahua or met someone who has, those owners deserve a spot in heaven. Chihuahuas' are alpha to their core, and other animals that may exist in the house should fall in line, no matter the size of the other dog, they may win in a fight, but they are going to leave with some war wounds. Chihuahuas are potty trained but only when they want to be. They eat all day unless you lock up their food. Don't leave a garbage can unattended or not put away, unless you like cleaning up trash all over your house. Invest in a steam cleaner. It is quite possible that Riley the chihuahua was autistic (Not a joke, I looked it up, and it does exist within animals). She was extremely temperamental if you changed any of her routine and would respond with destruction or scent markings throughout the house. I can count on one hand how many times this dog has shown me affection (my wife could get it on command though), yet every night for the first 9 years of Rowan's life, this dog slept between my legs and would not sleep any other way.

My wife is a super mother, one who researches and puts her best foot forward on right and wrong for the betterment of our children. Rowan is the only biological son she has, but without a shadow of a doubt, she would sacrifice herself for Alex, my eldest son, as well. Rowan was not a family name, or one that we had longed to call a son if we had one. It was the name that we would both agree "wasn't bad" after telling each other the names we preferred individually were not great.

Breastfeeding was a must in this house, as it was the healthiest form of feeding for our child, and my wife loved all that went with the connection and bonding between her and our son. Rowan really loved to eat though. He would not fall asleep early, most times at 11pm, and then wake between 2am-3am (my wife would correct me on this if she had been present for this writing, because she swears to this day, he was an angel for 3 months, and then the mass feeding began). Sleep deprivation for new parents is not uncommon, and yes, I didn't sleep much anyway, but still, I had my hours of sleep that I consistently had. Apparently, those hours included 2am-3am. Breastfeeding from a father's point of view seems painful, and I can only imagine this assumption is correct, as my wife often would whisper scream, "Ow, Ow, Ow, Ow, Ow". Finally, one night, I don't know what came over me, but in a moment of exhaustion the sound "SHSSSHHH" escaped my lips. The minute it did, I scrunched my eyelids in hopes Angela didn't hear me. She did....

Later that morning, around 8am, as we met in the kitchen, both quiet from aftermath of the abusive but well-deserved words I received after my slip up, we made a rule;

What is said between the hours of 10pm-8am doesn't count.

As a father though, I was determined to beat the mental sleep abuse this child was putting me through. I didn't need much sleep. He had no idea who he was messing with. Did he? After his 2am feeding, he would wake between 5am-6am and that was my duty, so that my wife who had been up just 3 hours prior could get some sleep. The amount of breast pump pouches she created was more than enough for a school of children, so we were good to go. The problem was, he didn't fall back to sleep at 5am. He was up till at least noon, when my wife would take over, put him on her breast, and he would fall asleep soundly. A real treat, because not only did my wife get 8 hours solid sleep, but 2 hours to adjust to real life with his nap. What a rip off! At noon, I was awake for the day, or ready to go to work. This process lasted for some time, until one night, he fell asleep in our bed.

We have heard the horror stories of co-sleeping with an infant, and I was determined not to lose my place in bed next to my wife, especially because of the possibility of a tragic disaster, but at 2am, my wife let him latch on, and by this time, her nipples had been abused and toughened over the amount of feeding she had done, that the silent sounds of pain she had were gone. More importantly, Rowan fell asleep while feeding. He didn't make a sound. This was magical! The next day, we went to the store and bought bed bumpers, and I made the decision that I liked sleeping more than winning this battle, Rowan earned my place in bed, so to the basement couch I went, and the basement can be lonely (as most basements are) so I was followed by a companion. The damn chihuahua.

She took her place between my legs and snuggled into a ball. Basements are cold, and this little added body of warmth made it very comfortable. My big screen tv was downstairs and I have always been the kind of person who falls asleep to tv better than silence (my wife prefers a running fan. She's one of those "fan" people). 18 months I spent sleeping with this animal in the basement before Rowan accepted that he would sleep in his own bed, across the hall from his older brother, who was one of his favorite people in existence. When I returned to my bed, Riley decided this is where we were going, because now we were a team. Angela didn't like it at first, but as soon as Riley made it impossible to sleep any other way, my wife reverted to what we had with our toddler, sleep is better than winning.

So back to March 16th, 2020. That drive to work at 9am, hoping we were going to make it to March 18th before there was a complete lockdown, and realizing, it made all the sense in the world to not allow St. Patrick's Day to happen if you were going to prevent crowds. The radio announced that at 3pm, all restaurants would be unable to allow patrons, and citizens were asked to stay home at all costs if possible unless you were "essential", which took a while to understand what that meant. It was a weird time in our history. Scott was on a cruise (a cruise when they cancelled the NCAA tournament and a limit on capacity the weekend before to 50% for restaurants) and had no idea what was going on. He was due back March 15th, and just made it without being quarantined in Florida, which was a worry at the time.

Our staff was worried, and yet wanted to make it through March 17th, but insisted that Scott not work because of being on a cruise just the week before. He agreed when I was finally able to speak to him. The staff has never asked much of us in terms of demands. We have been very lucky and fortunate throughout the years (except for one gas-lighting door guy who I regret ever having employed) of having loyal, intelligent, kind, and respectful employees. It didn't matter anymore, because we were going to be closed. St. Patrick's Day was cancelled. The disappointment was easily outweighed by actual relief. Whether it was media driven, or factual, or debatable, or whatever side you fall on the Pandemic spectrum, the protocol was exhausting, and I was more than thankful to just have a definitive answer as to what we were going to have to do. I had it now, and the preparations to get through the day wasn't necessary anymore. It was over. They said 14 days, but even in that moment, I don't think anyone really thought it was going to be over in 2 weeks. The staff that came in to set up that morning took one last picture before we shut down. I bought each a pint, and we said our temporary goodbyes, and went home.

What was I going to do now? 2 weeks, no work, no vacation. Sitting home with no place to go. By this time the grocery stores had been ransacked and the shortage of toilet paper (remember that?) was a thing. I put on a pair of sweatpants, kissed my wife, and went back to sleep. The chihuahua joined me.

March 17th, 2020, was the first day of the lockdown. I slept in. I am sure a lot of it was depression of spending so much and not knowing what I was going to be able to recuperate with missing the busiest day of my year. I am also sure a lot of it was that I was emotionally exhausted with trying to motivate a team of people who quite honestly, were going above and beyond when the government and media thought they should be at home. I was thankful for them and am thankful to this day for who they are.

Then there was the idea, that I wasn't sure what to do at home either. We could go outside, but it was frowned upon to see other families in the neighborhood. We had a 7-year-old who now needed us to be his playmates as well as his parents because he couldn't see his friends. We had to learn virtual schooling. Life is easy when you have choices, and most of the time I chose to be at home with my family anyway, but take away any sort of options, and it feels suffocating.

Day 1 was surreal because of the process and "what now?" scenario. I spent a good portion on social media seeing what others were doing and that helped, until you ran in to the anxiety of people wanting to force their opinions of "wear a mask, don't wear a mask, stay inside, go outside and hike, but stay away from others, listen to the government, the government is lying, etc."

The next morning, while scrolling through my news feed, I did a thing. I posted a short message.

*"Day 2....*

*I miss my job"*

58 likes... 14 comments....

That was how I was going to pass time. I was going to journal my days until this was over. It was only going to be 2 weeks. 14 days of posts? No problem! It would be fun! That's how this journey began.

## An Understanding Wife

*"Day 3…*

*So far today my wife has come out with great energy to get on a schedule which includes cleaning the house and working out…*

*I have finished a search and find puzzle with Rowan while eating a pepperoni and cheese roll-up I keep dipping in honey mustard…*

*My wife wants me to ration the mustard…*

*These are hard times…."*

My eldest son, who was working in a beer distribution center, loading and sorting stock, (He knew a guy who had inside connections… that guy was me) was considered an essential worker, so he wasn't asked to stay home. This was 3rd shift though, so he slept during the day, and thankfully his room was in the basement, so the rest of the family wasn't keeping him awake.

My wife has this undeniable iron will to meet tough times head on and turn them in to opportunities. We were going to be home for 2 weeks together. Angela created a schedule for us to follow, which included a dry erase board I was to hang up in the hallway that we could refer to if we weren't sure what the next task was going to be. The morning would consist of a spot cleaning of some place in the house, (usually beds made, dishes washed, laundry sorted) followed by a neighborhood walk, or drive to a hiking trail nearby for fresh air and exercise. This was followed by some sort of lunch and a late afternoon workout. After this there was family "down" time where we could play a board game or watch some tv, maybe read a book, before eventually getting a decent night sleep. In theory, it's a brilliant schedule to keep our 7-year-old busy and occupied while also getting things done and creating memories. In reality, all the stars must align for it to work.

The day started out positive, I was asked to hang the dry erase board up. Like any husband, I said,

"Do I have to do it right now?"

Like any wife, Angela gave me a look without saying words.

I had to do it right now.

After the dry erase board was put up, Angela had to organize it, so this gave Rowan and I time to our own devices. I tried to share my wife's energy and teach Rowan something new. At 7 years old, he still had not learned to ride a bike without training wheels. With little traffic in the subdivision and a large yard at my disposal, this seemed like as good a time as any.

He wasn't comfortable trying to ride on pavement just yet. The idea of falling and scraping himself was too great to concentrate past that. I had bought every padding imaginable to prevent this, but none the less, Rowan couldn't be convinced. In the back yard though, we had a large, grassy hill. He could get momentum as I pushed him down it, but also, not worry about falling with the softer ground below him. Rowan didn't want to do it, but I convinced him he could. On the count of 3, I would give him a push and down he would go, trying to hold his balance. We did this about 10 times, and each time we got to the count of 3, he would scream, "WAIT!"

This was my first attempt to create trust issues for my son and I, so on the 11th try, I pushed on 2, and down he went! Gliding, toward the bottom, but keeping his balance, I heard him yell,

"You went on 2, you were supposed to go on 3!"

I replied,

"Yeah, I do that sometimes. Bad at counting. Look though? You made it!"

Rowan was happy he made it but wasn't convinced I was telling the truth about being bad at counting. He did at least a dozen more downhills by himself and I looked on with pride that I had taught my son to ride a bike. However, I started to realize it was still early, and the grass was wet from the morning dew, tearing up parts of the hill which I was certain I would not be able to cover up from my wife.

My history of lawn maintenance during our relationship is not one to be proud of. Angela is a Certified Master Gardener and amateur landscaper. I was punished once for running over decorative grass (my wife claimed were Lilies) and the punishment was I wasn't allowed to cut the lawn ever again.

"Sorry?"

I said, confused as to how I am going to feel bad over that punishment.

I destroyed a bush in our yard by dumping water softener salt in its soil without thinking about what salt does to trees. Angela thought the citronella torch had dried it out for having blown up next to it. I thought I could probably go with that story for a while, but I had also killed some ivy on the other side of the yard with salt water as well, so it was just best to confess before she figures it out.

The hill though, technically Rowan's fault for riding his bike repeatedly on it, but I don't think my wife would see it that way. We stopped and went inside. I couldn't really make the tracks out from the back deck, so I think we were fine.

I took video of my efforts for "Father of the Year" candidacy, and my wife gave Rowan all the credit. Seemed less fair, he couldn't have done it without my guidance.

At this time though, we have been through lunch and missed exercising (darn) because the dry erase board organizing was more tedious than my wife expected. We did make it to a small hike in our back woods behind our house, and I am not a huge fan of small hikes. It's just a walk that gets your shoes dirty.

The rest of the afternoon seemed like we were going to have to do more chores, and I have become a Master of avoiding such things. I have a full-proof plan on how to distract my wife before she ever realizes what has happened, and by then, its usually too late, and even better if she never figures out, I have created a sabotage.

Angela loves to take pictures. She loves looking through them, creating albums, and reminiscing. If ever I have a need or desire to get out of actual housework, I need to plant a box of photos, or a stray album anywhere near her workspace. Maybe a sleeve or two she hasn't gotten to organizing correctly yet. This little move is a guaranteed time waster for at least an hour. Maybe more. You must be subtle about it though. During one of her bathroom breaks, maybe just have a photo prop on the floor as if it could have possibly fallen from a shelf that your wife won't be able to ignore. She'll go to clean it. Even with laser focus on a different task, those pictures are calling to her to be looked at. To be reminders of better times.

Day 3 ended with our trip to Disney World coming to memory. I played video games.

## The Oreo Dilemma

*"Day 4…*

*My wife continues her positive outlook, opening a waffle maker we received for Christmas and making everyone breakfast.*

*Rowan started using the Bluetooth speaker to listen to WWE wrestling themes, but has moved on to Imagine Dragons songs…*

*I can't begin to say how much more I would rather hear Wrestling theme songs…*

*I put jeans on today… not because they are comfortable, but because all my sweatpants are dirty…"*

*"Day 5…*

*My wife set up a camp out in the living room for the entire family. Rowan was thrilled. After Rowan fell asleep, my wife abandoned the campout for our comfy bedroom, leaving me alone with our 7-year-old and an ornery chihuahua. IKEA furniture is not made for comfort….*

*Laundry is done, which means fresh sweatpants… I just have to get the motivation to put them on…*

*Rowan has gotten past music in the morning. He is now on Netflix with Angry Birds 2. Still better than Imagine Dragons…*

*My wife has decided today is a day of rest… solidifying that she doesn't pay attention to what I have been doing, because my days have consisted of moving from refrigerator to couch to bed... At least we have Oreos to celebrate our isolation..."*

*"Day 6...*

*My wife is awake and singing while setting up online church for her and Rowan to attend...*

*I am debating on pizza for breakfast or just finishing the Oreos...*

*Rowan is back to listening to Imagine Dragons. He dreamt last night that my wife had 3 more babies. I hope I was involved in the process somehow...*

*I just found out that the State restaurant occupancy ban has been extended to April 13$^{th}$, so I need to buy more sweatpants...*

*Today I may use the treadmill. I haven't used it in at least 5 years...*

*I hope it still works..."*

*"Day 7...*

*My wife continues her positive outlook, waking up and getting on something called Zoom for a live workout, and even getting our youngest son to participate...*

*With rumors of the State lockdown coming today, we decided it was best I go to Sam's Club for the "essentials", alone... without supervision.*

*I came back with a rotisserie chicken, bulk toilet paper, Nutella, and 5 BAGS OF SUPER SIZE SNACK CHIPS! Needless to say, I am not as great of a doomsday prepper as most would assume... my wife mumbled something when she saw what I bought, that she refused to repeat when I asked what she said...*

*She's going to go back out for healthier nutritional choices...*

*At least I got toilet paper..."*

When we found out that rules of lockdown were increasing to only necessary travel outside of your home, like most people, we did some bulk grocery shopping. My wife got essential stuff like canned beans, rice, toilet paper, etc. Stuff we really needed. I had gone prior to this but did it wrong. During this time, I generally get junk food which I hide under her healthy vegetables and responsible nourishment. For whatever reason, I had a craving for Oreo cookies.

Fun fact, for many people who communicated with me during this time, I am not the biggest Oreo fan. I like them just fine. For store bought cookies, they absolutely are in the debate for best packaged cookie.

However,

Angela loves Oreos. They are her weakness, and if you present a double stuff Oreo, I venture to say, she has no control to resist its temptation.

I hid a mega pack under the broccoli and baby carrots. The next day, my eldest son had come up from his basement dwelling. He was hungry and looking through the fridge. This reminded me that I had gotten the Oreos and wanted to get them before he did.

Alex is 20 years old. He's a full-bearded mountain of a man, taking after his late grandfather. He will present you with a cocky arrogance, much like his father (sorry), but the interior that not many people get to see is soft, and kind. If you see that side, you have earned his trust. Something he doesn't give out easily. He's loyal, and funny, smart, and creative. He also has inherited his father's love for food and trying new things. I treat him more as a man than my son these days, and I explain this now, because the conversation over these Oreos goes down a dark path.

As I passed him in the kitchen, on my way to the snack HUB (that's a thing in this house), I grabbed the MEGA pack of Oreos. There were 4 remaining. 4... The day after we went shopping. I turned to Alex, and quietly asked, so that Rowan couldn't hear me from the other room,

"Motherf#@ker, did you eat all of these?!"

Shocked, Alex responded,

"I didn't even know we had these"

BULL$H!IT!",

I quickly and offensively said,

"Dad, it wasn't me.", Alex replied.

"Rowan, come here!", I called.

Rowan came over from his action figures,

Rowan: "Yeah?"

Me: "Did you eat the Oreos?"

Rowan, innocently looking at me with a straightforward answer,

"Yes."

Me: "You did?"

Rowan: "Yes"

Me: "How many did you eat?"

Rowan, counting his fingers, looks up at me,

"Five".

Me: "You had a lot more than Five."

Rowan, counting again, but more slowly,

"No, Five. I had Five."

It is at this moment, that I realize, the entire time, my wife has been washing dishes not 10 feet from us, in complete silence.

All of us turn our heads, ever so slightly towards the kitchen sink.

"Honey?", I went to ask.

“I don’t want to talk about it. You know I love Oreos.”,

never turning to face us, in shame, was my wife.

I went back to my couch, lying with disappointment that I only had 4 Oreos to eat from a Mega pack, but smiling at the same time. The next time, I would have to be more secretive about where I store these magical chocolate sandwich cookies.

## The House Flood

*"Day 8...*

*My wife doesn't have 30lb. weights to do her workout, so she enlisted Rowan and I to take a walk around the neighborhood... There is a fine line between compromise and obedience in marriage... I hate walking... I did it anyway...*

*We are officially out of Oreos... We were out the first day... I bought another pack... We are out again...*

*Rowan is currently negotiating video game time with my wife... Negotiations are not going well for him... I am Switzerland in this... It's much safer...*

*I am pretty sure I can open all 5 of these bags of Super-size chips and my wife will still love me...*

*I'm like 70% sure...*

*I have been able to avoid any real home projects up to this point, but I think my luck is running out. Something will be cleaned today, and it will involve my participation...*

*It's probably a good day to wear jeans. I see the garage getting cleaned out. It seems like the most likely area of the house to clean while you are in a pandemic shutdown of society...*

*Happy Tuesday (I think it's Tuesday?)"*

*"Day 9...*

*My wife's positive approach to quarantine 2020 continues. Waking up and doing another Zoom workout, which I have decided is basically FaceTime with a bunch of people who want to work out together...*

*I will stick to Xbox...*

*Our friend let us borrow their carpet steamer... My wife is preparing the living room and Rowan's bedroom for deep cleaning today... we will not be able to walk on either carpeted areas...*

*We are being quarantined during a quarantine...*

*I woke up this morning knowing my diet hasn't been up to par this week, and am currently in denial that I may be gaining weight... I suck my stomach in when I go past a mirror... I think I still got it...*

*Our family took a 6-week sign language course at the elementary school. My wife tries to sign things to me that she wants me to avoid having Rowan do... he understands her... I don't... whatever it is, I have a feeling it involves not giving him anymore sugar...*

*We were supposed to go to Asylum Lake today to "walk" some more... at least LEGO Masters is on tonight....*

*Happy Wednesday."*

*"Day 10…*

*I just watched "The Mighty Ducks" with Rowan… We made a bet on the final game… I took the Ducks… Rowan was super confident I was wrong… The movie is named, "The Mighty Ducks" … I love 7-year-old logic… There are sequels to this movie… I think I can use this bet at least 2 more times…*

*D&W Market sends me emails that are titled, "Last Chance to Save…" I am starting to believe them…*

*Every day at 11:30am, Rowan reminds me that he would be at recess right now… it's 11:38am… he would have been at recess for 8 minutes already… at least that's what he says… It has been a while since Rowan has played with a kid his age… I have to give him credit, because he has to settle for me and my wife… and let's face it… my wife is an adult…*

*Posting that I ran out of Oreos proved to be a blessing in disguise. 2 different neighbors brought over 3 family-size packs… I should be good till tomorrow at least…*

*My wife finished off a Sam's Club bottle of Sangria before bed and still made it up for Bible study group at 6:30am AND made a Christmas morning-size breakfast for everyone…*

*I continue to be amazed by her positive outlook and active approach, but there has to be a breaking point… we are out of Sangria…*

*The sun keeps peeking out, so I am going to stain some trim. I might even be able to put it up today…*

*All I have is time…"*

*"Day 11…*

*How on earth do the Kardashians have a show that has lasted for 18 seasons?*

*A friend of ours asked if she could come over so her kids could use the bathroom because they weren't close to home… my wife's biggest worry was if it looked clean enough… I didn't care…*

*I need to shave but I will need to shave tomorrow too… so I'm not in a hurry…*

*False alarm… her kids didn't have to go… my wife cleaned the bathroom anyway…*

*Time to put up the trim… I have no idea how to use an air compressor…*

*My wife gave away a pack of Oreos…"*

When Angela and I moved in to our first home in 2004, after 3 years or renting, our first major purchase was a treadmill. Most people may assume that it wasn't used to its fullest potential, if they follow any part of my lifestyle, but for its first 5 years, it was used almost daily. Our first home was what some may consider a "starter" home, and my wife told me she could see us there for 5 years. I don't relate well to change, and that little starter home lasted for 12 years, until one day I came home, and my wife had a realtor at our dining room table. We were moving; or she was, I had a choice, although not a very hard one.

We started looking for a new house, and like most couples, we had a wish list of things; a large lot, out-buildings, a basement we could turn in to a "man cave", and an inground swimming pool. If we could get all those things, or at least a portion of them, it would be fantastic. Our house sold faster than we thought it would, and in the process, we were having a hard time finding a house now that we were on limited time and in our price range. If it had a pool, it seemed to have a small yard. If it had out-buildings, it was a fixer upper. If it had everything, it was much further from the pub than we wanted to drive each day.

Angela thought we may want to rent month-to-month at our old apartment complex until we found what we were looking for, but at the time, Alex was 16, and having 3 bedrooms right on top of each other with one central shared room seemed like it would be a nightmare for our psychological health. Teenagers want their space, and parents need it. Plus, renting a 3-bedroom apartment was double what our monthly mortgage payment was, and I am classically cheap.

In the 2 weeks we had to make our decision, we researched and visited over 50 homes, before we found the home we moved to. The house we chose was listed for less than it was valued for, because it needed a lot of cosmetic updating. It had double the square footage of our previous home. The lot behind it was vacant land that had never been built on, and to this day, it has created what appears to be a large lot, although our next-door neighbors own it. It didn't have an inground pool, or out-buildings. It did have a very large walk-out basement with a workshop and living space larger than the house we called home for the last 12 years. The biggest surprise was that 3 of Angela's Bible study friends lived a block over from us. The chances of moving unexpectedly close to 3 different families you are friends with is a God send. With a limited amount of time to spare, we decided we would have to forego our wish list and make an offer on a house we felt most comfortable with, and this house seemed to be the best fit.

2 weeks after move-in, I went to my basement, which was wall-to-wall 1980's wood paneling, and sat in my Lazy Boy. Looking around, and planning in my head for an exercise room to put the treadmill and a man cave to put my television, I mumbled to myself,

"I can live with this for a couple years."

The next day, the largest rainstorm in our neighborhood in years occurred (or so the neighbor's say), and the sump pump in the basement did not work. The basement flooded and my comment to which God himself must have been listening, was no more. I would have to reconstruct it now. After calling in an excavation company to pump out all the standing water, and my home insurance not covering much for flood damage outside of a faulty sump pump, I decided I would do the demolition work myself. Rowan was 3 at the time and came down to help me. I used a hammer and a wedge to lift the first piece of wood paneling off the drywall and discovered, this was not the first flood this basement had experienced. From floor to ceiling, a black mold had gathered. Not knowing if this was dangerous or not, and whether I should be calling my realtor to let them know what we were not disclosed from the previous owner. Our home was owned by the mother of our next-door neighbors. Thinking about not having a fight with them only 2 weeks after moving in, and by all accounts, they were really nice neighbors, we decided to not involve any legal claims against their mother. I took Rowan upstairs and told my wife she needed to make arrangements to go somewhere with Rowan for the week. Alex was fine staying with his friends, and Riley was afraid to come downstairs, leaving me to do work. I went to Home Depot, got a painter's full body suit and mask, a mold kit, and gloves. I called a garbage company to drop off a dumpster in my driveway and away I went at the demolition.

The basement was 1700 square feet of wood paneling, old insulation, and carpet. I had a garden cart I would fill with debris, drag it up the hill to the front driveway, and dump it in the dumpster. I did this with a full body suit, a ventilation mask, and my adidas samba classics for shoes in the middle of August. Summers in Michigan can be hot, and this was no exception. The neighborhood must have thought I was watching a lot of "Breaking Bad" and possibly creating a Meth lab. I would wave often with the suit on, and most people turned away as if they didn't see me.

As I approached the end of day 2 of demolition, I came to a piece of dry wall that was brand new under a mold covered wood panel. I surmised that the furnace was replaced, being brought through this part of the basement and new dry wall was put up, and the paneling was reapplied. In my head, I had been giving the previous owner the benefit of the doubt that they didn't know the mold existed, but this was proof they did. Directly above this, in the open ceiling, was a bare wire that was left to breathe in the floorboards. Grabbing it from the taped center, you can imagine my surprise when I moved it and it hit the metal plumbing and sparked. It was live! I was furious and thankful that my family wasn't in the house, because the choice words I spoke to myself would have made a sailor blush.

The next day, I received the results of whether the mold was toxic or harmful, even though I was working so closely with it already. It was not. It was unusual to see in a basement, as it was normally seen in swamps and marshes, but going years without being treated, I can see why my new basement was swampy. Angela had made plans to spend the week with her mother at a lake house they rented, so I had to get the basement up to a deconstructed position. At the end of day 3, all the demolition was done, and I had filled an entire long-haul dumpster with my little garden cart time and time again, all by myself. I had the sump pump fixed, I treated the walls with stain and water-resistant plasma and built drywall frames with mold and mildew resistant panels. Angela came home with Rowan at the end of the week, and over the course of 2 months, we created a brand-new living space in the basement. I wired all the home theatre equipment through a wall into a hidden room and mounted our big screen television. I built a bar to store all of our licensed beer glassware we have collected over the years of owning Shakespeare's, and there are a ton of those. We got a sectional couch with a storage coffee table for seasonal blankets. Some light for Summer, some heavy for Winter. We restored our wood burning fireplace and bought a barstool table to seat 8 to go in front of it.

Then off the side, in a separate, yet open, room, I created the gym, complete with fridge for water and protein shakes, a mounted television and oscillating fan, a tread climber, a weight machine, and last but not least, our treadmill. The treadmill is 18 years old as of this writing, and it has seen better days, but we got our money's worth from it, because my wife has a positive outlook on getting in shape.

## How Angela & I met

*"Day 12…*

*It's rainy… Rowan and I have spent a good portion of the morning playing video games…*

*He wears a headset and thinks I can't hear what he says because he can't hear me…*

*Talking trash is not his strong suite… phrases like, "Come to Papa", or "Take that you overgrown Decepticon" have been said. However, he wasn't doing well, and loudly, the comment, "That's Bullshit!" just came out… I looked at him as any good father would do and said, "What did you say?"*

*He looked confused… how could I hear him? He was wearing a headset… I am not supposed to have the ability to hear with him having a headset on… His response was acceptable.*

*"I didn't know you could hear me. I will only say that in my head now, not out loud."*

*I should probably do the same… because the comment, "Don't tell your mother", hasn't worked well for me…"*

*"Day 13…*

*After finishing 4 family-size packs of Oreos, it seemed like a good idea to my wife for me to take up jogging this morning… it was nice at 8am… clear skies, 56 degrees… that was until we decided to jog…*

*Wind from everywhere, cloudy skies and 52 degrees... my shoes didn't fit right... Can't we just "briskly" walk? Who does this for fun? They have problems, not us... isn't church starting soon? 12 minutes later, I can say we started our day with a "jog" ...*

*Speaking of Church... my wife has been using "Facebook Watch" to attend... I don't watch with her... God speaks to me in different ways... just now, he let me hear my wife pray to him to help her from "swearing like a sailor." I appreciate that so much...*

*I went to the store today to get Tzatziki sauce for Gyros at lunch... there were Oreos... I just kept walking by... self-control makes me want to swear like a sailor...*

*I never did find the Tzatziki sauce....*

*Sweatpants are deceiving because of their elastic waist band. If only everything in the world had an elastic waist band- feel to it...*

*Happy Sunday everyone."*

*"Day 14...*

*Contrary to popular belief, my wife's enthusiastic nature will not be destroyed by me... but our 7-year-old might be the culprit...*

*Little boys like to make the highest frequency sounds and noises and he knows the exact decibel to drive my wife crazy...*

*Plus, he loves to ask her questions and make statements...*

*"Mom, I got a bloody nose and my blood tastes and smells like pennies. That was a long time ago though."*

*"Mom, there is a movie on Netflix called Big Fat Liar."*

*"Mom, can I eat Doritos and Cheetos if I finish my carrots?"*

*"Mom, Shawn Michaels WWE theme song is called Sexy Boy and that means handsome. Daddy let me listen to it."*

*The last one made me giggle even though he sold me out... Happy Monday."*

*"Day 15...*

*My wife and I did a workout video because I skipped "jogging" today... tomorrow, I will find a way to skip the video...*

*I hid a pack of candy bars and some breaded goat cheese bites to cook later...*

*I haven't used up all of my Netflix choices because I am conserving them... the Tiger King is on my radar though....*

*After working out, my wife asked me how here hair looks... I told her it was fine... she looked in the mirror, disgustedly and said, "Quarantine fine".*

*We went to the grocery store briefly, and my wife is complaining about the amount of frozen section grocery store-bought Crab Rangoons there are in the package...*

*I think this may be the day where her positivity takes a turn..."*

Angela and I met at a Target store I was working at over 20 years ago. She needed a filing cabinet, and her best friend and roommate was my co-worker. I helped her carry it to her car. We would run in to each other from time to time after, and when I took a job a local college bar, I got her a job as a bartender. Something she had always wanted to do.

When I was finally graduating with a business degree, dealing with a messy breakup, 6 months prior, and moving back to the East side of the Michigan to be an investment consultant, I came back one last weekend to finish moving my belongings and say goodbye to all the people I called friends for the last 6 years of my life.

Angela and I had always talked about hanging out after work, and it never came to be, until that final trip. She was working, and I asked her if she was getting cut soon (a term for restaurant workers when they are asked if they would like to leave early from their shift). She was. She went home and changed, came back, and we hung out for the rest of the night, with an old roommate of mine at a house they were staying at. It was a Ritzy place, and Angela and I spent a lot of time touring the home while my friend and his fiancé fought in the kitchen. To this day, my wife and I like to go to open houses for sale to see what's out there. As the night was winding up, I still had keys to my apartment, and we weren't tired. Our first movie was "When a Stranger Calls" we rented at some 24-hour video store. The original film (because they remade it) had one Iconic scene,

"Have you checked the children's room?",

but the rest of it was like watching paint dry. We fell asleep, and eventually just went to bed in my old room, which was weird, because here we were sharing a bed, and we hadn't even kissed. The next morning our first meal together was breakfast at a Cracker Barrel. We held hands while walking through their General Store, but still, no kiss. I went back to the East Side unsure of what that just was, and soon after, she sent me flowers to my work. Red and Yellow roses with a card that stated,

"Yellow is for the friendship; Red is for the possibilities."

From then on, I knew, this was worth pursuing, and I have never regretted doing so. It took 3 weeks of talking and getting to really know each other on a different level, including building up the importance of a first kiss before it actually happened. I think of my wife and those first few moments and in my head, I compare it to the meeting Ewen McGregor and Alison Lohman had in the movie, "Big Fish" where time stood still as he saw her for the first time. I am a romantic at heart but also a realist. If you ask me my opinion on the term "soulmates", my heart wants to say it exists, but my head is skeptical. I have never regretted moving in with Angela 4 months after our first kiss, and it was the right thing for us to do.

People can give you life advice on too fast, too slow, get to know each other, make a move, don't make a move, etc. The only real advice that matters is what makes you happy in any given moment. Making a commitment to someone is not easy. My heart believed this was my soulmate, and now my head does too.

## Alex... "Go back in time"

*"Day 16...*

*Our dog has recently been diagnosed with Diabetes... Rowan, not really knowing what diabetes is, made a song about it while chasing the dog around the house... if you hear him singing, "I love diabetes", don't judge me as a parent... judge my wife...*

*My wife is making homemade seed Pods out of empty toilet paper rolls for our garden... I married above my pay grade... we will survive an apocalypse...*

*I am running low on salt and vinegar chips... they are the superior chip flavor...*

*My eldest son pays me for the car insurance I have him on... he told me he hasn't paid me for last month because he doesn't want to handle physical cash during this pandemic... he will get it to me after everything has cleared up...*

*The older I get, the more I realize it wasn't that my mother didn't know what I was up to, it was that she was just too tired to call me out on my stories... needless to say, he will have to put gloves on, but he's going to pay me.*

*I have an idea for a short movie today, and just realized my phone has a movie making app. This is happening, although my wife refuses to star in it...*

*I must go on a bike ride today... there appears to be a negative impact on my life by teaching Rowan to ride his bike... I went from jogging to a fitness video, to bike riding... there is no escape from physical fitness in this household...."*

*"Day 17...*

*The more days I go with slip on pants and t-shirts, the harder it's going to be to remember how to button up shirts and put on a belt...*

*I am supposed to be teaching Rowan school work during this time, but the schedule always seems to say "recess' when I take over... he did turn the light off in his bedroom though... so at least I am conserving energy... science...*

*Rowan has gone a while without playing with a friend his age... I must give him credit, because he must settle for me and my wife, and let's face it, my wife is an adult...*

*Rowan wants to ride his bike again today... My thighs are sore... How on earth did I do this every day as a kid?*

*I miss them.... Happy Thursday."*

The chihuahua was 12 years old at this time, and she started drinking an insane amount of water and could never quench her thirst. She still weighed enough, had an appetite, regularly went to the bathroom (inside and outside the house) and played with her toys. However, something was off, and we took her in where they diagnosed her with diabetes. They told us she would go blind and that we would have to give her insulin injections twice a day. The idea of giving this horrible animal a shot and not losing a finger was my biggest worry. At first, my wife would give her the needle, and I would hold her, but Angela didn't like being the "poker", so we switched. I had no problem with it, and Riley truly trusted my wife, which made her less squirmy. It worked almost immediately, and the over-drinking and panting stopped. She was sort of herself again but looking older. The color had left small patches of her fur where it turned white. She was now a senior dog. Where did the time go?

I have spent a good portion of my time on social media making videos as proof of how horrible this dog is. They are all over my accounts if you don't believe me. I have had plenty of dogs throughout my life. All loving and fun and caring. Except for Riley, she was the worst.

Alex hasn't left a debt unpaid with me. He may take longer to get it to me sometimes, but he pays it. I have always taken pride in the fact he has integrity. Growing up, Alex was split time between two households till he was 12 years old. He then came to live with Angela and I full time. The lessons I have learned as a father I can attribute to him solely.

I wasn't sure I would want to be a father, and Alex was a surprise for me. I was just finishing my bachelor's degree at Western Michigan, majoring in business administration and finance. I wanted to be a Stockbroker, or so I thought. My senior year, going into my last semester, Alex's mother became pregnant, and I had choices to make.

I was always worried about not having enough income to support a family, and at 23 years old, I didn't have a job that would pay to have one. I decided my last semester at WMU, I would have to take classes all day Tuesday's and Thursday's, working my full-time job in the mornings at Target, and then getting a second nighttime job at Buffalo Wild Wings. I did most of my studying there during the day because it wasn't very busy between 1pm and 4pm, and I got to know the owners well. They offered me a job, and backtracking, this is how I met my business partner Scott.

You never know where life is going to take you, and I do believe in destiny vs. desire. I stayed at this job, eventually leaving Target after Alex was born, graduating during the Summer of 2000, and applied for jobs I went to school for. 6 months after graduating, I was offered a job on the East side of the state, and Alex's mother didn't want to move, which was ok because we were not very compatible. Our relationship as a couple was over, and I made the move, commuting every Thursday back to Kalamazoo to pick Alex up, bring him back to Livonia, where I was raised, and then turning right around each Saturday to bring him back to Kalamazoo. I did this commute for well over a year, even after having moved in with Angela, watching our car rack up an insane amount of wear and tear, and working at a job I discovered wasn't what I had hoped it would be.

Scott and I kept in touch during this whole time working on getting a bar open, which wouldn't have been a thought if I hadn't gotten that second job with him. I had never dreamed of owning a bar or working in a restaurant. Yet, it felt so familiar and comfortable. Alex's existence shaped the bulk of my occupational life. It's funny how you become what you become, and sometimes it's because of one instance in your life.

Angela and I moved back to Kalamazoo after Scott and I signed to lease the Shakespeare building. I remember Angela drove the moving van (she is a much better driver than me) and Alex and I drove the car to Kalamazoo like we had done so many Saturdays before, but this time, we were staying. No more long commutes.

Angela and I found an apartment with nature trails, free canoes for residents, an indoor/outdoor pool with a hot tub. Alex's mother's house was 10 minutes from us, and life was getting easier.

The first 10 years of Alex's life, we were as close as a father and son could be. He often would spend extended days with us now, calling his mother to ask if he could, and she more often than not, would let him. He was the greatest friend I could ever ask for, yet my son, so he looked to me for guidance and protection. I tried to teach him things I learned and grew up enjoying, like video games and soccer. He loved both, but he became addicted as most kids do, to screen time, and as a father I failed to limit the amount of screen intake. I think a deep portion of parenthood is dealing with regret, and I have plenty of it.

At 12, Alex was into his pre-teen years and argumentative would be a good descriptive word. He fought with his mother here and there, which I thought would work out as he got older. There have been pockets of time where Alex and his mother spent getting along, and even talking, but it usually ends with a chapter of no-contact. When he turned 13, that is where I was not prepared for "tough love", and advanced punishments, which I most certainly regret not doing. I have always felt guilty as his father, that I could have done things better for him, and tried to make up for that with material things. I was always supportive and spoke often of proud moments I had for Alex, but as time went on, iPods, iPads, smart phones, and video games became an overwhelming addiction that I should have contained. We stopped talking, and he stopped participating with us as parents. Angela and Alex had a rough road of relating to each other, and if there was ever a dark time in my marriage, it was this time.

Teenagers are almost intolerable, and they wear you down. I don't think my son thinks I am stupid enough to believe some of the stories he came up with, but maybe. After a while, you just get tired of the fight. You always love them, but the anxiety of "what did I do wrong" as a parent becomes overwhelming and I just fell into a depression of sorts that I had never experienced. If you asked me how I grade myself in life, I would say I am an honor student in most cases. I have a successful marriage, I am self-employed, I am a college graduate, and I love my mother. If you asked me how I was as a father to my teenage son, I was a struggling "C" student with tutoring.

Alex told me he didn't remember most of the good times of his childhood, or vacations we did, or holidays at our home. I often hope he was just telling this story, because it wasn't cool to reminisce about them as a teenager, but I am not sure, and he has never said otherwise. He once told me that he hated me, and that he always just put on an act of love.

"Don't feel bad about it though, because I hate everyone.", he said.

This was a time I know that he was at his darkest and refused to let anyone help him (Not family, and not a professional counselor), and I know that he was in a bad place, and I as much as I try and see life through his eyes, I didn't have 2 separate households with 2 separate ideologies of parenting like he did, and that has to be a little maddening for anyone. Angela once told me she felt he pushed his mother away originally because he wanted consistency. 1 household to call home. 1 bedroom. 1 kitchen. 1 holiday season. It's a logical theory and might explain a portion of why he and his mother were so estranged, but only Alex knows the answers to why we weren't as close as we were. If there is one thing, I wish I could undo, it is being told I am hated by the person I loved more than anyone else in the world.

That cut to the core, and to this very day, I have never truly healed from it, and if I am being honest with myself, it is my fault for not being more strict as a father. I wanted my buddy back. As an adult, years don't seem long, but as a kid, you develop past your parents, and it takes a while to come around, if you ever do. What seemed like yesterday, playing "The Legend of Zelda: Wind Waker" on a rainy day, must have felt like ancient history to Alex. He was a teenager acting out, and I am not the first person to have had their child say "I hate you" to them.

I often think I should talk to someone professional about it, because I can't process through it and get back to what we once had as father and son, but time is endless and as it goes on it will help the bad memories fade away. At least that is what I am hoping for, because what Alex says he doesn't have a good memory of are my most cherished memories, and now when I think of them, I am really sad. I wish time would move faster, and that my boy would tell me I was his best friend.

Alex is 23 years old as of this typing, and I can say I feel he's come very far. He has gotten a full-time job in cell phone sales, has his own apartment with his girlfriend, and most importantly, he smiles, and as his father, that's all I will ever want. He and Angela speak often when he calls the house about life and it is so comforting to see that. I don't spend Friday nights making Tollhouse chocolate chip cookies and playing video games with him and calling it "Boys night", while my wife was at work. Instead, I get calls asking for advice, which he sometimes takes.

He will always be my boy, but the little guy who used to sing "Ring of Fire" on repeat during long car rides is gone. I can't tell you how often I whisper the words "Go back in time" in my head, when Alex visits my house or when he is about to leave. I have such a strong desire to relive a portion of life where I was at one of my happiest. That was with Alex, from his birth to 10 years old.

## Video Games

*"Day 18…*

*My wife participates in something I like to call the "Mom Tax". This is where if you have fries, or a drink, or a chicken tender, slice of pizza, etc. Mom gets to take a bite/sip without asking… she is entitled… I believe this is why my eldest son eats downstairs…*

*I didn't realize my love for purchasing non-essential things until I started disciplining myself not to… Rowan was watching cartoons this morning and an "As seen on TV" add came on for these miracle bedsheets. They aren't cotton. They are soft, and they fit over any size mattress without making them look too big or too small… sounds amazing…I didn't order them… adulting is hard….*

*My wife is in the garden, waiting for me to come help plant onions… I can see her using a claw to till the soil… I said I was feeding our 7-year-old… I am posting this…*

*For the 5$^{th}$ day in a row, I have to ride a bike… I haven't ridden a bike 5 days in a row for over 30 years… needless to say, my tailbone and inner thighs hate this idea…*

*I don't think I'm such a bad husband because my wife has only done "day drinking" once since the shutdown… I would have predicted so many more days being married to me…"*

*"Day 19…*

*My wife and I have this unspoken game where we like to get songs stuck in each other's heads… I was able to get the song "Next Time I Fall in Love" by Peter Cetera and Amy Grant stuck in her head... my Peter Cetera impression is on point, but I may be a contender in a bad karaoke contest...*

*My wife has 4 siblings... they have a text chain going on since the pandemic started... it is the highlight of my wife's day... she smiles and dances around the house after each exchange....*

*Rowan and I started playing "Animal Crossing". to explain this game to anyone would make you seem silly, but the addiction is real... I can't wait to fish and catch butterflies that I sell to an owl, who hates butterflies...*

*Trying to make lunch today and speak to my wife about it and she's not answering the questions I ask her... If your spouse ever responds to you with, "I'm listening", they most certainly are not, in fact, listening...*

*My plan today was to clean my workshop in the basement but instead, I'm going to build a workshop in Animal Crossing... its almost the same thing... A Raccoon gave me the blueprints..."*

*"Day 20...*

*My wife thinks of something funny to say in her head and then never says it because she can't stop laughing at her own joke...*

*Her laugh is a mix between Burt Reynolds in "Smoky and the Bandit" and the dog from Hanna Barbara cartoons in the 80's... it's incredible...*

*I tend to laugh more at her reaction than when she actually tells the joke she thought of... she then exclaims to me that I am so lucky I married such a funny person... It's a fair trade off I suppose...*

*I had an idea to make "John Wick: the prequel" where I just film me playing with my dog all day... my eldest son thought it was funny...*

*I haven't purchased Oreos in almost a week, but Doritos is another question.... I have gotten plenty of those...*

*Sweatpants still fit.... Happy Sunday."*

*"Day 21...*

*My wife had plans to spread mulch in the garden and be done by noon. It is 12:45pm, I have been building frames for the garden and my wife looks to be planning more construction... I guess the mulch was a clever ploy... at least the chihuahua is with me barking at everyone that walks by...*

*The owl opened a museum today in Animal Crossing... I sure hope I don't miss the ribbon cutting ceremony due to my unexpected real life garden work...*

*Lunch consists of leftovers from all the cooking we have been doing at home... I hate leftovers unless its Mexican or Chinese food... I didn't make either of those... guess I will make a hotdog...*

*I have 2 pairs of Adidas Samba Classics and I accidentally stepped in dog crap in the yard on the right foot of one pair and the left foot of another pair... so now I have a clean shoe for each pair... that's practical...*

*I have never been off of work for 3 weeks in my entire life... I can say it is not for me...*

*Happy Monday"*

Let's talk about "Animal Crossing". The people at Nintendo made the virtual village and society which is a great demonstration of capitalism. I never understood its appeal, until I was without a job for an extended period. This game saved me from insanity and depression. I was without a purpose, not being able to work, in a place that I co-founded and built with blood, sweat and tears.

In this game though, there are daily tasks that are real time based. It follows a 24-hour clock relating to the time zone you live in. I have to dig up money once a day. I can replant the money and a money tree grows in full a few days later. I can sell fish at the farmer's market. There is a jerk of a raccoon named Tom Nook who posts as the mayor and rules with an iron fist. There is fishing and bringing what you caught to the Aquarium for donation. Over time as you earn money you can upgrade your house in size and stature. You can spend a lot of time recruiting other animals to come live on your island. Tom Nook takes all the credit, but that's what most politicians do. I haven't played the game since the lockdown ended but waking up with a routine helped make the transition from lazy to productive and that felt pretty great.

I love video games. The first time I can remember being introduced to them was at the age of 5. Christmas morning. I am the baby of 2 other siblings by a 9- and 11-year age gap. My brother is a left-brained person. Engineer by trade. Quick witted, but mostly quiet and not the most emotionally forward person. When he unwrapped the present with the Atari 2600 in it and immediately kissed and hugged my mother with such joy, I knew this was a big deal. It felt like we had 20 games that morning, and it was great to just keep playing them hour after hour on our 19-inch color television. I mastered Activision classics like “Mega-Mania” and “Pitfall”. “River Raid” and “Elevator Action” were my favorites. This was the beginning of what has become a lifelong hobby and as an adult, there isn’t a platform I don’t own. I have made friends with the “GameStop” manager, and he always makes sure I get on the list when there are pre-orders for new consoles.

Video games, especially today, are like interactive movies and books. Gamers know the map of the world as if it is their own, and that is credit to the developers. “Red Dead Redemption” is a fantastic experience for imagining you’re a cowboy in the Old West. Or “Assassins Creed” for so many different backdrops, like Pirates, or Vikings, or Ancient Egypt.

I’m the type of gamer my eldest son calls a “Completionist”, where I have to have all of the side trophies, missions, weapons, collectibles, outfits, etc. in my inventory before I quit playing. As my pandemic gaming journey continued, I was especially addicted to “Immortals: Fenyx Rising”, which was a very underrated game, similar to that of "The Legend of Zelda" but done for the Xbox and PlayStation gaming audience. I completed every part of the game which is about Greek Mythology. If you haven't played it, and you like games like the "Zelda" series, I highly recommend it.

I know that in the coming days of the pandemic, I wrote more about my experience with "Animal Crossing", so this is just the preview.

I have always appreciated that my wife looks at my hobbies and lets me be me. She married a nerd, with a decent personality and average appearance. She could have done better.

## My Mother

*"Day 22...*

*The day started out with the idea that I should jog around the block while Rowan rode his bike, then a sensible breakfast and lunch followed by a healthy dinner... the idea was nice...*

*The day really started out with me sitting in a massive bean bag chair while playing Animal Crossing, skipping breakfast, and getting Little Caesar's for lunch... my wife took the dog on a walk and ate Sushi... she has great discipline when I don't destroy it with chocolate sandwich cookies...*

*Rowan and I played soccer in the backyard... My wife asked me to stop scoring... It amazes me when I take it easy that 3 goals from him turns in to 17 on his counting scale... I suppose I lost, and should be a better math teacher...*

*I don't consider my diet "Carb Loading" at this point... I consider it second winter meal planning... at least Hallmark still plays Christmas movies...*

*Rowan keeps talking trash about my apparent loss... I am not sure it was worth it to listen to my wife... she doesn't read these posts anyway... I think I'm safe...*

*Happy Tuesday"*

*"Day 23...*

*My wife informed me that spouses are invited to do Zoom workouts with her fit body boot camp... so I did...*

*For 30 minutes I was able to become preoccupied with other distractions which included looking for weights, an exercise ball, and water...*

*The 5 minutes I did workout was entertaining, because I hid behind my wife as we ran in place... she was going side to side as if we were in a car chase... I am sure my footsteps were distracting, and she must have felt chased... This is role playing at this stage of our lives...*

*I set up a Fowling set in the backyard I received from Molson Canadian as a promo at the pub... it's a bowling/football combination game... I don't get its appeal...*

*I set up my Jack Daniels Cornhole boards instead... My 7-year-old is much better at this game... my wife isn't here to stop me from scoring... he won't be bragging today of any false victories...*

*I bought Ben & Jerry's S'mores ice cream... It is made with chocolate sandwich cookies... good thing I worked out this morning...*

*Happy Wednesday..."*

*"Day 24…*

*After an 8-hour day of gardening, my wife has decided to take a break and wear stretchy pants all day while being lazy… I am being as quiet as possible not to change this, because I am quite content avoiding housework…*

*My mother called this morning… when you get older, I suppose you like to discuss your demise with your children in a joking way… she was insistent when it's her time she expects us to "burn her and get on with life.", my wife, not missing a beat, says, "so we will throw you a surprise roast, got it." This is a brilliantly placed dark joke and I am so proud I married her…*

*My hair is longer than it has been in 20 years… so today I am going to shave it off… I think I will let Rowan do it…*

*I continue to purchase chips, and my wife has noticed and put a rule in place that no new chip bags can be opened till the other has been finished… but sometimes you want more than one… so I am going to ignore the rules… or play dumb… or I didn't hear her… or blame either of my sons…*

*When it comes down to it… I am eating salt and vinegar chips and Doritos at the same time…*

*Happy Thursday."*

*"Day 25…*

*Today is my 10th wedding anniversary… my wife asked last night before bed that I get up and work out during her*

*Zoom workout... I was up and in shorts ready to go!... she slept in... Happy Anniversary to me!!*

*We were supposed to be on a cruise right now... my back up plan was a bottle of Sam's Club Sangria... our neighbors felt differently...*

*They made signs complete with balloons, a basket of champagne with actual glasses, and a chocolate cheesecake...*

*Our neighbors are the best husband my wife could ask for...*

*Rowan is addicted to the "Big Show Show" on Netflix... it's kind of like Full House or Family Matters... It's garbage and entertaining at the same time...*

*I haven't shaved my head yet... maybe today... I will look like a new person... I hope he's better looking... and taller...*

*If you are friends with my wife, feel free to send her a sympathy post... she is 10 years into this marriage, and I am sure I have at least 30 years left... Happy Friday."*

My mother is my rock. When she was 36, she went to the family doctor, thinking she may have cancer, because she wasn't feeling well, and at that visit, they told her she was pregnant with me. She loves to tell that story and finish with the joke,

"No, please say it's a tumor."

I get my sense of humor from this lady. I was 9 years younger than my brother and 11 years younger than my sister when I was born. Quite an age gap, and for the most part, after the first 10 years of my life, I was living in an "only child" household. My father passed on from a stroke when I was 4. I don't remember much about him. Little things like when he came home from work tired and let me step all over him like a jungle gym. Or the smell of cigarettes because he was a smoker. He was quiet, and reserved, at least I think he was, but I can't remember the sound of his voice or any memory of bonding with him. I know this; my mother truly loved him. When he passed, she dated a few years later, but briefly, and never serious. She decided it was best to raise me without the possibility of a failed relationship. For anyone who thinks that children need a father/mother figure in their lives to be raised successfully, they don't. They need 1 strong parent, who can handle both roles. My mother is 4'11". Her stature has never been imposing. However, if I had a choice of people to walk down a dark alley with if ever presented with such a scenario, my mother is my choice, hands down. I was raised safely, and never doubted that I was taken care of. She is the strongest person I have ever met.

## My Sister & Holiday Mascots

*"Day 26...*

*The number of times I have heard the sentence, "Dad, lets wrestle.", Is equivalent to the number of times I hear the kitchen printer at work go off with an order, which is infinite... I hear it in my sleep sometimes...*

*It's my sister's wedding anniversary today... she wished us a happy anniversary via text and my wife seemed to remember it was her anniversary today... if I have to remember dates of anniversaries outside of my own, there is going to be a lot of disappointed people...*

*Our dog has stopped eating breakfast, so we were told to use peanut butter in her food... she eats it... it makes her thirsty... I take her out every 2 hours each night now... it's not awesome...*

*My wife, as cheerful as ever, has come out of the bedroom singing her high school production of "Oklahoma", with dance choreography in sequence... Oklahoma is a terrible musical... so far, the highlight of the day..."*

*"Day 27...*

*7:30am...after migrating to the couch because of a certain chihuahua during the night, Rowan has woken up to exclaim the Easter Bunny has been here...I hid 16 eggs... but I was tired... so from the comfort of my bean bag bed, when he was having trouble finding eggs, I would ask if he had checked certain places... sure enough, there was always an egg... my kid thinks I'm a genius... even in my sleep-deprived mental state...*

*I'm running out of Netflix shows... Prime shows... Hulu shows... HBO Max shows... it only took 27 days...*

*Rowan has moved on from play wrestling... instead he tries to knock me off my bean bag into the shark-infested carpet... but I outweigh him.... When he is about to go on the carpet, he asks if I remember the good times we had... his imagination is a little too real, and I feel bad... so I don't throw him off... he then tickles me off and I die... survival of the fittest, I guess...*

*My wife can't decide on which project to do so she has now started 3... they are all half done... as much as I avoid housework, I can't stand half-finished projects... I think coaching her is a bad idea though... maybe I should help? Ha! Never mind...*

*My Instapot has a recipe for a lava cake... it's an 8 quart Instapot... I'm going to be a while....*

*This is the most bizarre Easter Sunday I have ever experienced..."*

*"Day 28...*

*Mondays during this quarantine have been like a New Year's Day resolution... I have intentions to start a new fitness routine, make healthier meals, put on a decent outfit, maybe start a new skill I have always wanted to do... instead it's cold, the dog made me take her out to pee so sweatpants it is, and candy for breakfast...but next Monday, I'm on it...*

*I don't like jellybeans all that much, but you wouldn't know it if you saw my diet the last 2 days...*

*I don't know how to use my Instapot so I just hit the slow cooker setting... chicken will be ready sometime this week...*

*My neighbors have something in their garage window that when I see a glimpse of it from my kitchen window, it looks like a person... I mentioned this to them... this morning, I noticed they put eyes on it...*

*I'm going to teach Rowan how to tie his shoes today... I should have started yesterday with the Easter theme because I still do Bunny ears with the laces...*

*My wife is avoiding me... I know this because I have been playing video games for over an hour and the question, "Are you busy?" hasn't taken place... It is kind of a silly question...."*

*"Day 29...*

*The people on the show "Doomsday Preppers" are probably thrilled to say "I told you so..."*

*Rowan is playing with his wrestling action figures, and I eavesdropped on him saying "It's hard times, brothers"*

*Why I find this so funny is an example of quarantine hysteria...*

*I have turned into the retired old man who looks out the window and complains about cars who have temporarily parked on the street, or wonders what the neighbors are doing outside in the cold, or just asking for that dog-walker to not pick up the crap in my yard... try me...*

*My wife has maintained a sense of positivity longer than any human should... until dealing with the unemployment office... she then asks questions to me, and I try and help and she rolls her eyes at me like I said the most obvious thing... she calls her friend, who answers the questions with the same response but she's a genius... they then talk about bathing suit weather and a nicer future...*

*We try and feed Rowan healthy meals each day... but I can't tell you how many times "come get your chicken tenders and fries" have left my mouth in the past 29 days... he always gets raw carrots...so there's that...*

*I have run out of my current stash of chips, and have talked Rowan out of most of his Reese's eggs... I have no other need to go to the store... so I will remain out of chips... and I will finish his eggs...*

*I believe my "flight or fight" reaction would lean more towards fight, because flight would require me to move at this point... and this bean bag chair is all I need... Then again, fighting seems like a lot of cardio....*

*It's Tuesday which means tomorrow is garbage day... the highlight of the day will be taking the trash to the curb..."*

My sister's wedding anniversary is the day after mine, but her marriage year is much further back than Angela and me. Kathy, my sister, is the eldest child. 11 years my senior and the wild child of the 3 of us. She was once a hair stylist with 80's punk rock hair and fashion shows. Then she moved on to playing professional darts in Vegas with her husband of around 30 years? I really am not sure. If my mother is my ultimate protector, my sister isn't far behind. She has no kids of her own, but never forgets a birthday for any of her nieces or nephews. She was the first person I called when I knew Alex was unexpectedly coming into this world. I live across the State, away from the family, and I am secure with that, because my sister is close to my mother. She takes care of all the family dilemmas and organizes all the important things for my mother.

She's a great sister, and I know if I ever need her, she will drop everything and be there for me. I won't remember her wedding anniversary though. It is what it is.

This quarantine diary details the last year that Rowan believed in the holiday mascots. We were on a car ride the following year to his school's open house when he asked how the Easter Bunny got eggs? For whatever reason, the idea of the Easter Bunny has always annoyed me. I love hiding eggs, and coloring them, and setting up a basket, but really, the whole setup of a religious holiday to have a mascot bunny who hides chicken eggs with some sort of basket reward at the end is crazy to me. I have never spent the time to research its origins, and I guess I am not that interested to do so now. I answered his question with this,

"Do you think there is such thing as a Bunny who hides eggs?"

Rowan was quiet. I wasn't sure if I just spoiled a part of his childhood or if he was contemplating the answer. I had a few seconds of panic, wishing I could have pulled the question back, but then he answered,

"No, I think it's kind of silly. Why a bunny?"

"Right?",

I was thrilled he saw it my way.

But then....

Rowan had a light bulb go off in his head.

"Is Santa real? How about the Tooth Fairy? Leprechauns?"

All at once, I realized I wanted the Bunny to be called out, but now I was going to lose the rest of them. A huge part of growing up was over. He seemed pleased to know the truth. My wife was happy to see he had matured enough to know as well.

I was kind of crushed. My youngest son had outgrown the existence of make-believe holiday mascots. In that moment, it was more about what I lost than Rowan, and it made me sad.

I have referred to the existence of a giant bean bag chair I own. For years, I had been researching giant bean bag chairs I could have as a gaming seat for ultimate comfort. They are as big as a love seat and hold their shape like memory foam. However, they can be expensive for a bean bag chair and finding the right space to put them in can be tricky.

In February of 2020, I finally pulled the trigger without discussing with my wife and ordered a Sumo Lounge. It came the last week of the month. In a box I believe was 36x36 inches. Upon opening it, the directions said it would take a full week to inflate to its ultimate form. My wife calmly looked at my purchase and asked the smart question,

"Where is it going to go?"

This is why I didn't tell her about it. It doesn't fit anywhere practical in the house. I unloaded the box in the middle of the living room, and to this day, this is where the bean bag stays. It is absolutely out of place. My wife is a good sport.

After the week had gone by, and the bean bag had inflated to the size it is supposed to be, we were able to sit on it. The chihuahua claimed it as her own. She wasn't sharing, so we had to fight. We came to an agreement that she could still sleep between my legs on it, but I was going to use it.

The bean bag became a point of interest early in its life with our household. The last couple days of February, my eldest son came home from work sick. So sick that he asked my wife for a head massage because he couldn't get rid of the headache he had. She did this for him, and he went to bed. My wife decided to deep clean the house that night while I was at soccer. During that time, she got equally sick and couldn't hold her head up. While at my game, at halftime, it hit me. I was also dizzy and having trouble staying in the game. Whatever he brought home, we all were feeling it. I went home from the game, took a shower and went to bed. Rowan checked on me right before. 2 hours later, he was equally ill.

Our symptoms were chills, and tiredness. Slight fevers with flu-like stomach pains. Stuffy congestion and shortness of breath. Rowan had a fever of 103 for 7 days until it broke. Angela had breathing issues for 3 weeks. Alex had vomiting issues. I had a fever and fatigue.

I spent most of the week on the bean bag with the chihuahua. When I wasn't on it, my wife was. If she wasn't on it, Rowan was. The chihuahua shared with all of us.

Like most people who went through the pandemic shutdown, we all hypothesize that this was COVID-19, we just didn't know it because it wasn't an everyday topic on major media channels. We were a week or two early.

If anything good came about this possible case of COVID-19 with our family, besides it being a minor case, it's that the bean bag was now acceptable in our household.

The chihuahua was thrilled.

## Star Wars Rankings

*"Day 30...*

*For the last week, I have been putting shorts on under my sweatpants in order to motivate myself to exercise... the first day, it worked great... the second day... it worked... day 3-7... I ate a lot of chips...*

*Watching the current season of "America's Got Talent" with Rowan and I have discovered that Rowan doesn't understand comedians... there was a comedian who had underdeveloped arms, and his joke was that he used to juggle chainsaws... Rowan was horrified exclaiming,*

*"He must have been really bad at that..."*

*I had to get pet food and vegetables at the store... so this gave me a replenish my chip stash... I didn't buy anymore Oreos... I think if I did, my wife would be less than thrilled with me...*

*Speaking of my wife... I forgot that she had plans to exercise this afternoon... even though she told me more times than I can count... and I brought "Chick-Fil-A" home... during her workout... I don't know if you can be an enabler with food, but I dare say I might be the world champ at it...*

*My dog loves getting her insulin shot, because she gets treats after... if she could, she would give the shots to herself...*

*I have gotten to the point of paranoia where I am checking my throat to see if its sore, even though it's not, it could be discomforted?*

*My right ear is warm? Or was I lying on a pillow too long? Wait? Did I lay on that ear?*

*I feel like I must cough. Do I have to cough? Is it dry in here? Is it going to be a dry cough?*

*As least I'm not congested. I could probably breathe a little easier though, couldn't I?"*

*"Day 31…*

*My 7-year-old woke up asking to watch "The Phantom Menace" and proceeded to argue with me that it is the superior Star Wars film… he's 7, and I know this, but illogical arguments are unacceptable… he ended the argument with, "You're still the best Dad, for now…"*

*I guess he's taking applications…*

*My wife is determined to eat all of our leftovers by creating new meals with them… I know all about Pork fried rice, but ham fried rice just sounds off… anyway… that's what's for lunch….*

*While cleaning out my workshop, I have had some fluorescent tube bulbs standing in the corner… for the past 4 years… my wife said that was a bad place for them… much later after that comment she knocked them over and they broke… hearing, "I told you so" doesn't have the same impact when you aren't the one who broke them… I don't think this counts as her being right, am I wrong?*

*I don't know why I always wear my black sweatpants when we are working in a dusty environment, but I can say, it looks as if I have been working extremely hard so I kind of like the façade...*

*Thursday is usually co-ed soccer with my team...*

*I really miss those people..."*

*"Day 32...*

*The Star Wars Saga continues in the Vadella household... Rowan was not impressed with Rogue One, which is ridiculous, because it is the best Star Wars movie since the original trilogy...*

*He exclaimed at the end,*

*"They all died!"*

*Maybe I should have explained its premise first... Preparation in these cases is important... However, if he bashes "Empire", he's getting grounded...*

*My wife changed the words of Howard Jones' beloved 80's song, "Everlasting Love" to "I need you to eat your vegetables" which she sang to Rowan... she laughed at her own joke and pointed out how lucky I am as a spouse to have married her...*

*All the Reese's eggs are gone...*

*My wife threw out the remaining jellybeans for my own good...*

*I have no desire to build a snow man... so I am hoping Rowan doesn't remember that we can do that with snow...*

*my wife, on the other hand, wants to get our bathing suits on and run outside... if she's protesting the weather, I don't think it will work... It's Friday... another weekend begins..."*

*"Day 33...*

*In an attempt to cheat the system, I decided to eat all the sugary snacks in the house in one day so that I couldn't have anymore... there is a fine line between will power and laziness... I am sure we will need something at the store later to eat... and while I am there anyway...*

*Rowan saw a YouTube video where someone cut out the back of a giant bear and got in it to scare their mother... we have this bear... and he asked his mother if we could do this... she said no... this is the part where I debate if it's better to do something and ask for forgiveness later... plus, I have to find an unsuspecting victim now that he told his mother his plan... maybe Grandparents through Facetime...*

*We have moved on from watching Star Wars movies to playing LEGO Star Wars video games... much better than watching Episodes 1-3...*

*My wife has decided to re-visit using the dry erase board we purchased at the beginning of the lockdown for next week... sometimes it's nice to know that I am still a mystery to her... as will be the where-abouts of the dry erase board...*

*It's Saturday, in case you didn't know..."*

*"Day 34...*

*I found a Rice Krispy treat this morning... now I am pretty sure I got all the sugar out of the house... but I'll keep looking...*

*I looked at Rowan's huge stuffed bear to see if I could pull off getting him in it... the amount of stuffing and mess I would have to clean up outweighed my desire to prank my mother... probably for the best... she wouldn't find it as funny as I would...*

*I think I prefer cold, snowy weather during quarantine to warmer, sunny weather... it just seems more positive to stay inside...*

*Rowan has circled the block on his bike 29 times today... teaching him to ride his bike is the best accomplishment I have done since opening day at the pub... and I haven't had to ride around even once...*

*My wife had me put up a greenhouse today... it took 30 minutes, but I feel as if I have an excuse to take a break... for the rest of the day... I finished at 11am... probably should have just put my pajamas on right after...*

*The dry erase board hasn't been brought up yet, but my wife has been drinking coffee, so I have a feeling "we" are going to be super motivated to complete some tasks this evening...*

*I have lost the motivation to even think about cooking anymore at this point... and I am running out of chips...*

*Happy Sunday..."*

Making home cooked meals everyday was becoming exhausting. Alex used food delivery services daily during the lockdown. I never understood why anyone would pay so much extra to have a restaurant who doesn't deliver on their own, brought to you. He would order from places around town that I had never heard of, and this was my first experience learning about "Ghost Kitchens" which basically is a restaurant allowing another entity or using a different name to sell products out of their restaurant. There was a slider burger company that ran out of Texas Roadhouse, or a pizza company that ran out of Chuck E. Cheese. Most of the time, he felt ripped off to think he was getting a new chicken wing place only to find out it was Applebee's.

Then one day, I had just run out of all motivation to cook, and pizza had run its course as a choice for delivery. So, we explored Door Dash and ordered burgers from 5 Guys. For roughly $10 extra I didn't have to put on shoes, get in my car, and pick it up. Then the real bonus, I NEVER HAD TO SPEAK TO ANOTHER HUMAN BEING! I type in the order on the app, tell them to leave it at the door. No questions asked. AMAZING! We did this very often during the lockdown now, but not so much since. It is a nice service to have, for the times you are ultra-lazy, and I can't thank the creators of this idea more than I am right now.

Television has always been a bonding experience for me with family. When I was a kid, we watched "That's Incredible", or "Family Feud". When I was in college, it was "Who Wants to be a Millionaire?" When Angela and I started dating till the present we didn't miss a season of "Survivor". For times that we watched as a family,

"America's Got Talent" went a long way for us. We have gotten away from it since the pandemic and moved on to our new favorite, "Lego Masters", but the idea that we have something all of us can watch has helped create great family memories. Angela would always prefer that activities like Rock climbing or Hiking be in the forefront, but even so, I think she appreciates the breakdown of why a show or movie is so good.

We are a Star Wars family, at least to a casual extent. No, we don't have light sabers around the house, or décor per say, but we did own a cat named Wicket (Angela's cat, owned before we started dating, and one of the coolest facts about my interest in her was her love for Star Wars), for those of you in the know. It is of great importance that the movie order of greatest Star Wars film to least great Star Wars film goes as follows:

1. Empire Strikes Back
2. A New Hope
3. Return of the Jedi
4. Rogue One
5. The Force Awakens
6. The Last Jedi
7. Revenge of the Sith
8. Phantom Menace
9. The Rise of Skywalker
10. Solo
11. Attack of the Clones

It isn't a close debate, although some of you may disagree, but "Attack of the Clones" is a rotting pile of trash.

Discuss amongst yourselves.

## The Hipster Chipster

*"Day 35...*

*My wife woke up at 6:15am with the dog and our 7-year-old and let me sleep in... by that time she had already planned our day and it began with a bike ride 15 minutes after I woke...*

*I will take my early morning job back tomorrow, which consists of sleeping on the couch with the dog while Rowan plays...*

*Rowan started online school with his actual teacher today... every 30 seconds he gets up and tells me how the computer lesson gave him the wrong answer... apparently 14-8=8 according to him, and the computer can't convince him that it's 6...*

*Stupid computer...*

*I had to look up the definitions of a "verb" and "adjective" because I couldn't remember the difference...*

*I'm still not entirely sure I understand the difference...*

*Teachers are the most underappreciated/underpaid occupations in the United States... To all my friends who are teachers, I salute you. I recognize the magic that you do...*

*Now on to deep breaths and counting to 10 as I try and imitate your job and be a good parent...*

*Chicken tenders are for lunch... I ask my wife if she would like them on a bun or in a wrap, which leads her to repeat, "R-R-R RAP!" This happens periodically throughout the preparation of lunch... and she laughs every time...*

*I want to go back to bed...*

*I spanked my wife while she was doing dishes... Rowan heard it from the living room and came in to see who spanked who... he knows what a spank sounds like... I have to be less frisky during the day, I guess...*

*Rowan ran his bike into my car at the end of the bike ride... he said his brakes don't work... I checked them... they could stop a bus...*

*Stupid bike...*

*So far, this Monday has started out energetically, and I am not prepared..."*

*"Day 36...*

*Rowan's gym teacher sent an email with a link to her physical education lesson plan... it was a YouTube video... we started watching it... but there were other videos of cute kittens and puppies next to it... My wife should probably be the substitute teacher...*

*I set up a mini soccer field in the backyard and Rowan and I played 1v1... he had a diving save and claimed to "break his wrist" from his years of medical training... my wife bandaged it... suddenly, he has total mobility of his wrist... my wife should have been a Doctor... she has healing powers...*

*I think I may have ordered too many cookies... not because I can't eat them... but I don't even think I can justify the amount to the lady of the house... she has no idea how many... and I am positive she won't guess that I would order so many... even for me... I am going to play "the birthday card" on this one...*

*The computer continues to give Rowan all the wrong answers... even when I agree with the computer...*

*Stupid computer and Dad...*

*I am holding out hope that we can go back to work 5/1... I miss ordering beer for a living... Happy Tuesday..."*

*"Day 37...*

*Rowan's teacher had a class meeting set up for all the kids to interact... she's a really good teacher... she must not be as easily distracted by kitten videos as I am... She had the kids share their favorite book and after each one, she said, "Super fun!" I assume repetition is important, but I couldn't help but suggest to my wife that we can turn it into a drinking game... we could call it "Super Fun Happy Hour."*

*My wife ignored my suggestion...*

*Lately, the dog has been waking up around 3am to go to the bathroom followed by the cat to go outside at 4am... I usually have sweatpants at the end of the bed but with the excessive use of them, they are in in the wash a lot... I have this game called, "random pants" now... could be mine, could be my wife's... whatever I find is going on... yoga pants aren't as comfortable as you ladies suggest...*

*Animal Crossing is not a fun game... yet I play, every day, because it simulates work... I just found out that I have a little over a week to catch certain fish and bugs before they are gone because much like Netflix, things come and go in this world on a monthly basis... I hate this game... I have to go fishing and bug catching now... and this stupid raccoon takes advantage of me and my money to build his island and I am not compensated nearly enough... Like I said, it's kind of a job, and more realistic than necessary...*

*Rowan's favorite question of the week, "What can I do?" This is an obstacle because my wife limits tv and video games during the week and he can only play with action figures for so long before he wants to do something active, and he can't see his friends so that leaves me... I am sick of 1v1 soccer, but I win a lot, so at least I have that..."*

*"Day 38...*

*My hair has reached a point where I could play Danny DeVito's role in a remake of "Twins" opposite Patrick Dempsey... it's "McDreamy-esque", heavy on the McDonald's portion of it... that was a "Grey's Anatomy" reference... which I have seen every episode of until this season, and that was before the quarantine... no judgement...*

*My Mother-in-law spoils our kids at Christmas every year to the point where we can't possibly open all the gifts, so we spread them out through the year... this has come in handy this week... I opened and put together a night-vision shooting range... it held interest for a shorter length of time than I hoped it would... the floor is now lava... if he doesn't stay entertained, I am going to throw him in the lava...*

*My 7-year-old thinks it's hilarious to "sell me out" when I give him sugar while his mother isn't looking and tell her about it... my eldest boy never did this... he is the intellectually superior child... yes, I get a "look" from my wife, but the youngest boy no longer gets sugar for the rest of the day...*

*I decided to go through all of my sweatpants instead of rewashing all of my favorites so much... I don't understand why I own loose ankle pairs instead of only owning ankle huggers... I am 5'5" tall... all pants drag on the floor for me... and it's wet outside... this makes for uncomfortable socks...*

*My wife has been hiding in our bathroom... she is redoing the carpet cleaning since our chihuahua reclaimed them by peeing when we aren't looking... this dog is the devil..."*

My birthday is in late April, and I usually don't wait for my family to pick out the cake or ice cream for it. I was shopping at a Grand Opening of an Office Depot store, and they had this home baker passing out chocolate chip cookies she had made. There is a little cookie shop in the Petosky, Michigan area called "Tom's Mom's Cookies". The shop reminds me of "Hansel and Gretel" house, inviting with sugary goodness and not as dark as the German fairy tale (Look the original story up, it's very dark.). The shop is no bigger than a cubicle office, and they have 1 glass counter display with about a dozen different cookies to choose from. In my opinion, they are the perfect cookie. Soft on the inside, with crispy edges that aren't too crunchy and just the right amount of sweetness. The shop can only hold 3 customers at a time, making a line down the street almost daily. They were the best cookies I had ever had. Until I met this home baker.

Tara DeVries is the owner of "The Hipster Chipster Cookie Company". Why she was at an Office Depot handing out sample-size cookies is a mystery to me, but while I was shopping for printer ink and paper, if you offer me a free cookie, I will take it. It didn't cross my mind in the moment that this little rainbow chip cookie would be so fantastic, but I believe it was fate that I needed printer ink at this exact day they were handing out cookies.

I spoke to Tara briefly about it and told her about my love for "Tom's Mom's Cookies", and to my surprise, those cookies were her inspiration. It is quite possible she was buttering me up and didn't have a clue what "Tom's Mom's Cookies" were, but I like to think it made for a better story to the origin of her cookies.

I took Tara's business card, and months later, when it was close to my birthday, I ordered some. At the time, she had 8 different cookies to choose from, so I ordered a dozen of each. I didn't really do the math, but when I finally took the time to think about it, 96 cookies were probably not going to be a good idea to present to my wife. So, I didn't. I have said it to my wife many times, sugar is my mistress.

Realizing I had 8 dozen cookies coming soon, I planned to pick them up, and freeze them in the Chest freezer in the garage. They surely wouldn't be noticed there, and before we knew it, they would be gone, and no one would be the wiser on how many we had. The freezer was full of bone broth my wife had made at home. My wife is big on home remedies first before any prescribed medication. She makes her own Kombucha, and we have this brain-like creature living in a jar in our cupboard. You don't fake sick at our house. This is the medicine if you do.

I had nowhere to put these cookies, and I knew I was going to have to do something in order to not be in trouble. It kills me to say it, but the solution was to share with the neighbors. So, my wife and I went to 4 different neighbors houses, dropping off a variety box of cookies to each. In case they are reading this, you weren't given those cookies out of love. You were given those cookies out of a lack of preparation on my part. I do learn from my mistakes though.

I asked Tara to do a beer and cookie pairing at Shakespeare's during Kalamazoo Beer Week, and it got a nice reception. I tried to talk Tara into opening a store front for her cookies, even going so far as to offer to purchase a coffee shop and use her as the baked goods provider. She politely declined. Someday though, Tara, if you are reading this, I hope you do, because you make edible magic.

## Keto

*"Day 39...*

*I tried a new trick in order to exercise today... I put shorts on and didn't put sweatpants over them... I turned on the Xbox 360 Kinect workout, and proceeded to watch Rowan do it... I am so close to exercising; I can taste it...*

*I woke up with "New Kids on the Block" stuck in my head... in 19 years, my wife and I have never discussed how she despises them... I played it for Rowan on the house speaker... he asked to play it again... I had to say stop... but this is going to be stored in my memory bank under, "Things I do that annoy my wife."*

*It's a large folder...*

*Rowan started pouring a bottle of water into his workout cup... it started to get near the top... instead of stopping he just kept pouring in a panic saying, "there's too much!" All over the counter... it was just water... This should have been a teaching moment I had with him as an infant...*

*At least he knows the difference between verbs and adjectives...*

*I texted the cookie lady asking how I should pay her? ... She said I could write a check, cash, or Venmo... I texted back, "Either way you'll get paid.", but originally, autocorrect changed the word "paid" to "laid". I am thankful I caught this before I hit send... I would have thrown my phone out... and I don't think she would have delivered the cookies...*

*Stay at home extended to 5/15... I remember when I served beer and nachos for a living... good times... Have a safe weekend everyone."*

*"Day 40...*

*Rowan and I finished Star Wars: Episode 4 last night... this morning I asked him if "A New Hope" was better than "Phantom Menace"? His answer was irresponsible... so I told him he was grounded... he was so very confused and pleaded his case that "Return of the Jedi" was the best... although I disagree with that, it is an acceptable answer... so his grounding is under review...*

*After 6 dozen cookies showed up magically this morning, I could see the defeat in my wife's eyes, so I told her my plan was to share with the neighbors... she felt better about it... I am fantastic at this game called "Marriage".*

*A bonus to this quarantine is that only 1 person per family can be in a store at a time... and my wife couldn't help me because... anyway, I have 3 pints and 1 quart of ice cream, 74 cookies, 2lbs. of cheese, 6 tacos, a large nacho, a pizza, and breadsticks... lunch was great!*

*I must start thinking about dinner now...*

*It's time for LEGO Star Wars video gaming now... Rowan only gets to be Darth Maul... I know he is disappointed with not being allowed to be the other characters, but you must respect Han Solo to be Han Solo....*

*Happy Saturday..."*

*"Day 41…*

*My birthday… a day where I can get away with all the things I do normally but have to hide on the other days…*

*I ordered pizza and breadsticks… 2 days in a row… my wife started making ice cream cookie sandwiches with what was left of the cookies I ordered… I should be ashamed of what I ate… but…*

*Speaking of cookies… I can't decide if my neighbors like me or want to see me killed… my wife got a text that there was a package at the front door… I opened the door and picked it up… and my wife said, "That's Oreos! I can hear them!" 2 family-sized packages… she can hear them… is it really me that has the problem?*

*I went out to change the oil on my lawn mower and the across the street neighbor came over with a gift bag… 3 family-sized packs of Oreos! I am thrilled! I don't think my wife will be… I promise not to let myself go… starting tomorrow… it's Monday… I'll put shorts on under my sweatpants… that always almost works…*

*I had lavender ice cream today… with actual lavender… lavender seems like it might be healthy… so I ate healthy ice cream today…*

*Come to think of it, there were vegetables on the pizza too… so I had healthy pizza…*

*I am going to play Animal Crossing now… I still don't like the game… but I owe money to the raccoon… and I don't want him telling the porcupine who sells me clothes that I'm not good for it…"*

*"Day 42...*

*I woke up with the idea that this is the day to commit to getting back on track with my diet and exercise... I packaged and froze the remaining cookies for my birthday, except for the family-sized Oreos, and planned a bike ride with my 7-year-old...*

*There was a Transformers movie on, and I forgot to put shorts on under my sweatpants... to start getting ready dressed all over seems time consuming... so maybe next Monday I thought? No, this had to be the day! Enough was enough! I decided to work out in sweatpants, not shorts, while watching the Transformers movie... There are birthday cake Oreos and Dark chocolate Oreos, but I have to avoid the temptation...*

*My wife was motivated to continue working on her garden... she put her headphones on, and although I don't think she was listening to any music quite yet, I did hear her singing Kenny Rogers "The Gambler", but in a heavy metal style...*

*I am intrigued...*

*I got to a point of Animal Crossing where this stray dog came to the island and performed a rock concert... they rolled the credits... this is usually reserved for the end of a game, but after, the Raccoon, who, might actually be a squirrel, gave me construction plans to build roads while he said he was going to be more "hands off" but still collecting money... I hope there is a point in the game where the island becomes a publicly traded entity, and I can force him out...*

*I had to get vegetables at the store today, and I wore a bandana around my face because I lost my mask... it was very "Old West" of me... I didn't buy any junk food... we have enough...*

*I have to package and freeze these cookies now...*

*Happy Monday..."*

Over a month of not working, with no end in sight, and if I'm being honest, the recharge from 25 years of working overtime each week was welcomed with open arms now. I loved that it was extended and that I could continue with my new daily routine, which I had gotten used to. Rowan and I were always close, and I have always made time for my sons, but now it was as if I was a stay-at-home parent, and I didn't hate it. We ate breakfast, and took bike rides, and attended virtual school, and I played Animal Crossing daily to complete my tasks. I loved wearing sweatpants and relaxing and spending time with my wife. It was time to stop eating bad though.

Before the pandemic, I had 3 knee surgeries and a hip surgery, along with my sugary diet, I was gaining weight and became the heaviest I had ever been in my life. One day, while working, a customer I hadn't seen in a while made mention that I was looking "Hefty". I don't know why people think that you can say such a thing in a joking manner, but it is what it is. It was a wake-up call though, and I needed a change.

I have never loved exercise for the sake of exercise. Playing a sport with a purpose made sense to me, but running for fun? Or lifting weights so that my arms and legs would shake? No thanks. Researching the internet on supposed experts in the field of exercise, and most I found said 90% of the battle was eating right. If ever there was a time I would be set up for failure, it would be changing my diet drastically. I knew that I could give up some things or limit the intake of them at the very least, but a full change would be too drastic.

I had started Keto. A diet restricting your carb intake. I am not a health expert, and I will never claim to be, because eating bacon and burgers and cheese and limiting the intake of fruit and vegetables can't possibly be a healthy lifestyle alternative. I remember deciding one day to just read the carb count on food. Sugar was out, and that was going to be very tough. Bacon and Bratwurst though, I could eat all day, as long as I didn't have a sandwich with a regular bread, bun, or wrap. Ranch dressing and mayonnaise were on the menu. Ketchup was not, even the low-sugar variety. Canned whipped cream was sweet and a good alternative for sugar cravings, because it had very little carbohydrates. I remember the first 3 days just feeling so ill, almost flu-like from the sugar detox. My body was craving an insane amount of water, drinking continuously. Then on day 4, I felt lighter. I had more energy. This couldn't be from bacon, could it? I followed this diet for a while, determining that once I hit my goal weight, I would re-introduce fruit and vegetables and healthier alternatives to sugar and ween myself off greasy and fatty meats and cheeses as my only consumption. A little over 3 months and I was down 40 lbs.

The "cons" of Keto for me were the lack of variety. Pinterest had a lot of recipes, especially slow cooker meals for Keto, but you can only put a pig in a dress so much before you just accept its always going to be a pig. I was sick of bratwurst, and bacon, and chicken breast, and burgers without any real bread to go with them. I missed rice and beans. Keto worked for me in the sense of losing weight, but I am sure had I stayed on it permanently my heart wouldn't have thanked me.

## The Amazing Ab Belt

*"Day 43...*

*No matter how many times you take a chihuahua out to pee, they always have more than enough left to do it on your bedroom carpet...*

*While using a hose to clean patio furniture, always assign your 7-year-old to only turn the water on and off... handing him the hose guarantees you are getting wet...*

*I am in the market to purchase a "Crowler" system and found the right guy... so it looks like I might be canning draft beer for carry out at the pub whenever we re-open. Remembering how to do my job reminds me there is light at the end of the tunnel...*

*Teaching math today under the subject header, "Fact Families", my eldest son looks at each question and knows where they are leading to... my first grader understands what my eldest son is saying... I see 100 different possible answers... either I am artificial intelligence or the dumbest man in the house... I hate to lean towards the latter, but I will remind both of them that I still pay the bills...*

*My youngest son no longer tries to negotiate what schoolwork he needs to get done now... he tells me what he is going to do... he has not tried this approach with my wife... in the end, he does what his parents tell him... when it comes from my wife..."*

*"Day 44...*

*I have lost my motivation to be lazy and suggested to my wife we organize the living room shelving unit... she looked at me with an animalistic stare and told me of her plan to go through photos and books to get rid of for it... funny how the stare was for the idea of organization and not my clean, close shave...*

*I regained my motivation to be lazy halfway through... I figured the photo albums would distract my wife, but they didn't... it was a scheduled workout she had that got me out of organizing...*

*I realize that organizing is just moving stuff that needs to be thrown away to a different part of the house to be thrown away later...*

*Rowan wanted to go on a bike ride, and I would jog, but it was sprinkling... then I remembered this was the test to myself... so I went jogging in the rain... I ate a cookie when I got back as a reward...*

*Bob the cat asks to go outside often... when I let him and the weather isn't what he prefers, he looks back at me as if I did it... I think Bob would like to have a word with God on his choice of weather conditions...*

*I just realized the cookie I gave my 7-year-old had espresso chips in it instead of chocolate chips...*

*This could be interesting..."*

*"Day 45…*

*Now hear me out… I am never going to exercise willingly… however, passing my microwave today I remembered a pre-workout powder I purchased… so I read the directions… 2 scoops 30 minutes before you want to work out… do not exceed more than 2 servings a day… gummy worm flavor…*

*Who is working out twice a day that needs this? Show-offs!… all drinks are "pre-workout" for me, and if we are getting technical… you had me at gummy worm flavor… I drank it… and after I did, I started planking with my wife… I made it 2 minutes! If you don't plank, that's a lifetime! This stuff may work!*

*My wife puts on spa music when she does housework… the same music you would hear if you were in "pre-massage" mode… I don't see the correlation between housework and a massage, but my wife finds both relaxing apparently… and why does this music always have a flute? She went on a walk with Rowan…*

*I turned it off…*

*I did actual work for the pub today, getting recommendations for web designers… I responded to 14 emails… that seems like a lot after 6 weeks of doing nothing…*

*My wife came back from the walk… she wants to take a nap… she turned the spa music back on…*

*I think I will play Animal Crossing… I have some turnips to sell in the "Stalk" Market… Happy Thursday."*

*"Day 46...*

*The first day our 7-year-old has gotten punished and will write, "I will obey my parents" during this entire quarantine... my wife snuck away to exercise in the basement, leaving me to supervise the sentences... it is probably frowned upon that I play video games while he writes sentences and a poor management decision by my wife to leave me to supervise...*

*We went to a park today where skateboarding and bike riding were prohibited... we saw the same couple do both activities and Rowan's head was going to explode because they broke the law... twice... he wanted to tell on them... I wanted to say, "snitches get stitches" but my wife was there... and I don't think she would approve...*

*I snuck a cookie and ice cream as my lunch today... that isn't hard to keep away from your spouse, but to pull it off with a 7-year-old AND during a quarantine is ninja level skill...*

*We have 10 bags of mulch, and it's supposed to be a nice weather weekend... any ideas of procrastination or excuses are greatly appreciated..."*

It's obvious I don't enjoy exercising. I love short cuts to desired results though, and over the years, I have found a few that have helped me stay interested in getting in shape.

I love "As seen on TV" products. When Angela and I lived in our first house, with 1 bathroom, we would get home from closing the pub together at 3am, and I would let her shower first while I watched TV. The only thing on at the time, because this was before streaming platforms, were "As Seen on TV" commercials. Depending on how long my wife took to be done showering, resulted in if we were going to get something in the mail or not. I have ordered hamburger shapers, and pancake pans, and even hair removal systems, but the exercise equipment I have found on late night infomercials are some of my favorites.

One night, while flipping through channels, I came across an "Ab-builder" electronic belt. It had vibrating sensors with gel pads over them, attached to a spandex-like belt with Velcro fasteners for any waistline size. The model showed how the sensors expanded and retracted with a tightening sensation as if you were doing a sit up while in reality, you were laying on the couch watching TV, reading a book, doing housework, or grocery shopping, even doing desk work. The results showed washboard abs on a man and a woman who were obviously only using the belt and had never done a sit up in their life. In small writing under their muscular frames was the phrase, "Results not typical, and vary."

A lightbulb went off in my head. I would wear this belt, in secret, periodically throughout the day, for 6 weeks and not tell anyone. If suddenly I was getting a well-chiseled core, I would share with my wife the genius purchase I had made. She would try it, maybe want one of her own, and we would be beautiful people without having done 1 actual sit up. I ordered the deluxe set, with replacement gel pads for when the first batch would ultimately wear out. I paid the $100 plus processing and handling which was an additional $20 and waited for 4-6 weeks for my new work out gear to arrive, never telling a soul about what was coming in the mail. It arrived in an unmarked box, while Angela wasn't home, and I was able to hide it under our bed until later that evening, while my wife was at work bartending, I would take it on its maiden voyage.

Later that evening, I was watching TV and opened the box. The little digital insert for the belt required 4 AAA batteries. Yes, AAA batteries were going to give me an abdomen that Chris Hemsworth would be jealous of. The batteries were provided, which was nice. Classy even. I put the batteries in, attached the belt around my waist, and read the directions for settings. Taking things in moderation, the belt allowed for a scale of 1 to 100 on the threshold for which you can take. Deciding that I should really test my limits, I put the belt up to 100 and held the button till it turned on. I had forgotten to put on the gel covers for the sensors.

My skin felt an immediate burn of electric shock pulse through my stomach that was continuous and didn't let up for 20 seconds, with a 5 second delay between sets. To say it was painful would be an understatement, but not from the constant tightening. It was from my lack of remembering to finish reading the directions. I needed the gel pads. Each time I tried to take the belt off, it would shock me, and my hands would fall to my side. Eventually, mind over matter, I was able to pull the Velcro away and the belt fell to the ground. The hair on my belly where the sensors contacted was gone. In its place was a smooth, red irritation as if I had just waxed myself there.

Determined to not give up, I put the gel pads in place, reconnecting the belt to my waist, and again, turned it on to 100. The initial burning shock was gone, but the retraction of a constant sit up was equivalent to being hit in the stomach with a baseball bat. How can 4 AAA batteries do this?

I turned it off and re-adjusted the level to 30. Laying down on the bed while watching TV I fell asleep. Level 30 was like a cat trying to make a bed with their paws on your stomach. Comforting.

After a few days of adjusting the belt, I settled on level 60 as being a tolerant 20-minute workout. The belt contracts as if you are tightening your core before one of your friends jokingly slaps you in the stomach. I am not sure this was going to work as advertised. I was coming to terms with accepting that this belt would not be something I could tell my wife about, and that it wasn't going to give me a rock-hard abdomen.

A week later, my Sister-in-law, Tracy, came to visit us from the East Side. Tracy is my wife's only sister, and they have that sisterly relationship where they love each other and then want to kill each other from time to time. "Trace" has always been a lot of fun to have around, and she usually enjoys my crazy and questionably stupid antics. Angela was going to take her out with her best friends to a dance bar of some sort. They were getting ready in our one bathroom, and my wife was making conversation with her friends and sister about how I had just run over the lilies and wasn't allowed to mow the lawn anymore. This seemed as good a time as any to introduce my ab belt purchase to the family, since they were having a laugh at my expense anyway.

I went upstairs, grabbed my belt, put it on to make it completely visible, and went back down to the gathering of ladies who had now moved to the living room to talk. I made my way to the living room entrance, put my finger on the start button, jacked it up to 100, squinted my eyes, put my arms out at full extension and braced for the impact. With all eyes on me, and not one person sure what the hell was going on, my wife said,

"What are you doing?"

"OW! OW! OW! ",

I cried, as restricting shockwaves hit my stomach.

Five seconds went by,

"OW! OW! OW!",

it hit me again.

My wife now, clearly embarrassed by my show,

"What is this? Ted! What did you buy?",

I could feel the disappointment.

After about 3 rounds of laughter, I finally got the ab belt off, and explained what it was, to the intrigue of a room full of women who knew exactly what kind of a person I was and didn't need to hear the "Lawn Maintenance" incident. My wife kissed me on her way out, trying to hide the smirk she had, something she does when she finds me funny, but won't admit it.

Later that evening, as the bars closed, and I was up in bed, I heard the returning laughter of 4 slightly intoxicated women come home and attempt to put on the ab belt with the same results. I wish I had woken to see it, but all and all, although not used for its intended purpose, the ab belt's comical existence was $100 well spent.

## The Urinal

*"Day 47...*

*We are out of espresso chip cookies... I know this because my wife asked for one... and I ate all of them... even though I just put them in freezer storage... to get in better shape... but I am weak-minded... to say it mildly, my wife was... disappointed... but as you would expect she remained positive and said, "at least we have the pretzel cookies left" ... I ate all of those too...*

*Rowan is preparing for the apocalypse... he came inside with a handful of dandelions and said we could live on these if we ran out of money and food... he doesn't know about the cookies yet...*

*We went on a hiking trail today... Rowan got sweaty and asked if he could take a shower when we got home... I said showers are for morning and evenings, and to finish his day before taking one... he said some people take showers in the afternoon... and he wants to be one of those people... it's a logical argument...*

*I saw a construction packet for a backyard swing/firepit arena... complete with built-in projector screen... I was motivated to start this... but when Rowan wanted his trampoline up... and then we went hiking instead of constructing either of those... so I am just going to order Chipotle...*

*At least its shorts weather today...*

*Happy Saturday..."*

*"Day 48...*

*I put a trampoline up... 10 minutes after getting it up, Bob the cat got curious, and Rowan took that as an invitation to put him in an enclosed trampoline... my wife grounded Rowan from the trampoline...*

*To repay my wife's protectiveness, Bob joined her in her garden, and proceeded to go to the bathroom... annoyed, my wife critiqued his ability to bury his stuff... she told him he wasn't as good at it as our last cat...*

*The cookie lady sent me a picture of all the ingredients she purchased today... I doubt very much she sends these types of pictures to her other customers... so the espresso cookie dilemma is being fixed as we speak...*

*My neighbor offered me an Oberon after seeing me put up the trampoline... but I play this game every year at the pub to never be the person who pours an Oberon... It's a hard game to win... and I'm not losing on a trampoline construction...*

*And I don't dare tell my wife to pour it for me...*

*Happy Sunday..."*

*"Day 49...*

*Monday...*

*There is a fly in our house that taunts me and no matter how many times I try to swat him, he gets away...*

*I decided to show my wife the home I made in Animal Crossing... King-size bed, hardwood floors, bamboo walled bathroom... I was excited to show her my taste... she looked at it and slowly walked away... I can sort of see how pathetic this must seem through the eyes of a person who doesn't have to answer to a raccoon... plus, there was a urinal and a bidet, and I have never cleaned the bathrooms in our 19 years together...*

*The fly is taunting me now...*

*I picked up the espresso cookies from the cookie lady... I showed my wife and even stopped and got her a chili dog from the root beer stand... she ate them, but I know later she will not be happy with my kind gesture... and I might have to go on a walk or jog...*

*Damn, I can't catch this fly..."*

*"Day 50...*

*Checking my email, it appears I have signed up for Amazon Music Unlimited... I didn't do it... my wife wouldn't do it... Rowan told Alexa we would love to... all because he couldn't hear, "Toxic" by Brittany Spears unless he agreed to sign up... I must figure out parental controls on this speaker... Amazon finds ways to get my money...*

*Speaking of singing, my wife woke up practicing the bass in her voice... when I saw her, she said I wouldn't understand, I was never a performer... this continued through lunch when she broke out, "Drop it like it's Hot" Opera-style... this didn't require bass, it was more like Soprano... she has such range...*

*My wife decided to jump on the trampoline with Rowan... She pulled a muscle doing flips... we aren't in our 20's anymore... her singing stopped after this...*

*I froze the cookies last night to keep from eating all of them again... I defrosted them by lunchtime today...*

*I made tacos today... not because it's Tuesday or the 5th of May... Just because I would eat tacos everyday if I had the motivation to cook more...*

*I caught the fly... It's time to take out the trash..."*

Bell's Oberon is a Kalamazoo rite of passage. It signifies the first days of warm weather. It's a traditional wheat beer and was one of original flavors of the craft beer movement in Michigan. Customers started adding orange slices to it. For the longest time, Bell's didn't even offer oranges at their own Eccentric Café, but they came around to the idea.

In the first few years of Shakespeare's existence, customers deemed the seasonal release of Oberon, "Oberon Day", taking time off work to have the first pint. Bell's would open early on this day, get a decent head start, but because they had a line, and on Mondays at Shakespeare's, we ran $2.50 pints at the time, by days end, we would sell more Oberon than the actual brewery! I bragged to Larry Bell, the founder of Bell's about this once. I never outsold them again.

The first week we would average between 30-50 barrels of Oberon sold before the pandemic and at the height of Craft Beer's rise to excellence with the consumer. We sell a fraction of that the first week in the current climate, but it's still Oberon, and we still sell a lot.

I started this personal game to never physically pour a drop of Oberon if I can avoid doing so, as long as a customer was able to be served by any other bartender. The first few days of release, it's near impossible and I have lost this game almost immediately most years. In 2014, I made it to July 3rd, and lost, on a sample size pour. I had never made it any further until 2019. I successfully completed this game, and never poured a single drop. It is the only time I had won, and I have given up on the game now that I have achieved the goal. The pandemic started 2 weeks before 2020's Oberon release. It is quite possible my victory had cause for the world to go into disarray and shutdown.

As a bar owner, and anyone who works in the restaurant industry in Michigan, especially Kalamazoo, we have heard time and time again, "Oberon is not as good as last year" or "Oberon is better than last year". Oberon is brewed year-round and distributed in States that average 70 degrees in temperature or higher every day. It is the same batch year-to-year. I promise.

The firepit/projector was too big a project for me to attempt and gave me anxiety thinking about it. I did order a cheap projector from Groupon, complete with outdoor screen. The screen was a sheet, that I had to build posts for. The Projector was finicky at best. It would only work with certain shows, and sound quality was hard to improve, because it didn't have Bluetooth capabilities. I did have a wired outdoor speaker that we had never used until we got the projector. It wasn't great, but it was a neat little neighborhood gatherer. We watched some Disney movies and "Super Market Sweep" as a tester, but it really wasn't the biggest crowd pleaser. My wife wanted to watch "Jaws" while floating in the neighbor's pool. In theory, this was a great idea, but I will have to get a better projector, and it isn't at the top of my spending criteria.

Some people may think I waste money on unnecessary things, but in my head, they are worth the money. My wife was going out of town once, for a "Girl's trip." This was shortly after I had completed a bathroom install in our basement. I had left a spot across from the toilet open, that Angela thought I had done to create a Curio closet for towels and such.

I agreed, with a smile,

"Yeah, that's what it's for."

That wasn't what it was for.

I left the wall open, in the bathroom to my "Man Cave" so that I could get a full Urinal install. Rowan was a toddler by this time, and about to start potty training. I knew my wife would hate the urinal, so I had bullseye targets made to attach to the inside of the urinal to encourage proper potty training. This wouldn't be enough to convince her of its installation, so I weighed the option of "It's better to ask for forgiveness rather than permission." The Girl's Trip was the perfect weekend to have it done.

Jim the Plumber, who did all the work at the Pub, and one of my favorite people I have met professionally in all the years we were open. He was good to me, and he was good to my family. He was an honest, hard-working man, and I speak of him now in the past tense because he lost a battle to cancer. Jim did a lot of projects for me, from shower and water heater installs, to drain clearance. My wife loved him, even asking him to family dinner a couple of times. Riley the chihuahua did not, because the first day we flirted with the idea of a shock collar to control her barking, Jim was over. The second Riley barked at Jim, she felt the sting, but wasn't sure, so she barked again. She yelped out of fear rather than pain, but my wife didn't want to use the collar again. Riley was sure Jim did this to her, taking the heat off me for being a "Man" in her house, and this was enough to make me feel Jim was a good man.

I called Jim, and said,

"Hey, Angela is out of town Friday, so any chance you can come install an "in the floor" urinal Saturday morning?"

"Why in the floor? You can just hang it on the wall. Cheaper and easier to install.", Jim asked.

"I need it in the floor. Once it's done, it can't be undone.", I told him.

"Angela doesn't want it, does she?", Jim questioned.

"Of course, she doesn't. Silly question.", I replied.

"Well, it's your funeral, but I'll be there.", Jim said.

Working Friday, afternoon, I had to get home by 5 so that I had a chance to see my wife off, and prep Rowan and Alex for a Boys weekend. I was excited for the drive from work to home, knowing that as of tomorrow this time, I would be teaching an unsuspecting toddler how to practice peeing at a bullseye target. I had 2 days to perfect it so that the idea of the urinal was ok.

At 5:05 I turned down my street, and saw that my plumber was already in the driveway. He was unloading his tools. I had time to stop him and send him on his way if I hurried! Before I could turn in the driveway, it was too late, Angela saw Jim and popped out the front door.

"Hey, Jim, what are you doing here?", she asked.

"I'm here to install the urinal.", he told Angela.

She laughed,

"We aren't getting a urinal."

I could see Jim forgot that I wasn't telling my wife this, as he made eye contact with me, I saw the lightbulb go off in his head.

I got out of my car and never took my disappointed eyes off Jim. My wife called for me, calmly,

"Ted, can I talk to you for a second."

Never taking my eyes off Jim, I responded, defeatedly,

"Yes".

I went to my wife on the front steps, who looked me in the eyes and logically asked me 1 question,

“Hey, have you ever cleaned a bathroom in our 12 years together?”

“No.”,

with disappointment setting in, I surrendered.

“I think you know what to do.”,

my wife said softly, as she went back inside.

I turned to Jim,

“We aren’t getting a urinal”,

as I walked towards him.

“You blew it!”, I whispered.

I never did get a urinal.

## The World's Oldest Person

*"Day 51...*

*My wife hid dry groceries in our guest room closet the first week we were on quarantine... I have seen them, but forget about them every time I want to cook... it's probably for the best... because Kraft Macaroni and Cheese isn't the meal you should follow up with after using the word "healthy" eating... but I did just buy some butter... and I would hate for it to go bad...*

*I refroze the rest of the cookies and this time it is for real... magically, there was a lemon shortbread bar mix in the pantry... butter is a needed ingredient... so is lemon juice... and I don't have any... so I am safe from myself for the time being... but I do need to defrost burger for later... and it's under the cookies... 2 birds... 1 stone...*

*Rowan asked Alexa how old the oldest person is alive... I wondered why would that thought enter his head, and while I was wondering that, Alexa answered, and I missed the answer... I am super disappointed I didn't hear the answer, but I am at a point where I don't want my wife seeing me ask the same questions that my 7-year-old asks...*

*Teaching today has gone great... he's on a field trip... to the trampoline park... in the backyard..."*

*"Day 52...*

*My hair has reached the length of an aging boyband member who is begging cruise ships to hire him to perform...*

*My wife and I went on a walk around the neighborhood so that she could test her pulled leg muscle... she announced to Rowan it was a "Day Date" since he wasn't coming... she said this to people as we walked by them... my wife needs a date night...*

*The amount of ketchup that is consumed in this household is unheard of... Factor in that my eldest son isn't home to eat it and I don't eat it, that leaves my wife and youngest son... I have bought 3 family-size bottles since quarantine started...*

*We thought Rowan had appendicitis last night... his dramatization of pain was so convincing we wound up in the ER... come to find out, jumping for 3 days straight on a trampoline might cause the same symptoms...*

*The hospital was not busy, very efficient, and the nurses and doctors were happy and smiling... still, any hint of a sniffle I may have makes me think, "Is this it?" ... COVID-19 paranoia at its best...*

*Happy Thursday."*

*"Day 53...*

*After getting himself dressed, my wife told Rowan he looked handsome...he replied with a compliment, "You smell amazing Mom!", which made my wife smile... the kid already does better than me in the flattery department...*

*In case anyone was wondering, Hallmark is still playing Christmas movies... one of my friends mentioned that there would probably be a Christmas movie based on our current events... I swore there was already one titled, "Quarantined at Christmas", or "Christmas Quarantine". I was wrong... sort of...*

*First, there is a "Quarantined Christmas", it is a horror movie, low budget, probably for the best... Second, Jeffrey Dean Morgan is pitching the idea for a COVID-19 related Christmas movie... Yes, that's right, Negan from the Walking Dead... Not sure if Hallmark is involved though...*

*Looks like the whole family is going to start a Hunger Games marathon this weekend...*

*Sign of the times....*

*Happy Friday."*

*"Day 54...*

*I made the mistake of letting my 7-year-old know my mother's age... he now compares everything that is aging, old, or ancient to her... this morning, I sang the song, "When I'm 64" and when I got to the lyric, "will you still feed me?", he interrupted, "You can feed yourself! Yia-Yia is much older than 64 and she still feeds herself."*

*I put on jeans today... I don't have a scale, so this is how I could check to see if I gained weight... they aren't snug, so I am fine...*

*My wife likes to look for Morel mushrooms every year because she found one once in our driveway 5 years ago... we have never found one anywhere else, ever since... until today... I found one in the woods... my wife said I deserve a prize for finding it... this is foreplay in my house now...*

*Facebook ads introduced me to a cookie dough shop... I ordered some... it should be here next week... I didn't tell my wife... sugar is my mistress...*

*I can't decide if I should bonfire or continue our Hunger Games marathon with the second film tonight...*

*This is what Saturdays are like now...."*

On the list of "100 Known Verified Oldest People", the oldest person in history was Jeanne Calment of France, who lived from 1875-1997, and passed at the age of 122 years and 164 days. In interviews, Calment remembered selling colored pencils to Vincent Van Gogh and seeing the construction of the Eiffel Tower. However, demographers have speculated about the authenticity of her age. Russian Gerontologist, Valery Novoselov and Mathematician Nikolay Zak hypothesized that Jeanne died in 1934 and her daughter, Yvonne, born in 1898, assumed her mother's official identity, but many mainstream longevity experts consider the hypothesis weak. I looked it up, without my wife's knowledge as to not appear to be as curious as my 7-year-old.

Yia-Yia is Greek for Grandmother. My mother waited a long time to take the title, and she more than earned it. It is a weird transition as an adult to now refer to your mother as Yia-Yia when talking about her in conversation. I can only imagine the change for my mother was equally odd. My mother has never been a fan of sharing her age, and I have never been a fan of getting older. I believe a lot of my personality traits are directly linked to my mother, and I love her for them, but I try and own who I am when it comes to something I am not terribly proud of. Whether it came from her or not. My mother will always be my safe place, and she deserves to feel respected. Except for tiny jabs like telling her grandchildren her age.

I have always heard about the stereotypical "Dad-isms" like keeping track of the thermostat or turning lights off to save on the electric bill. Those things have never been an annoyance for me. I did learn about myself though, that the extra use of condiments that aren't proportionate to their intended meal side plates drives me crazy. My wife loved ranch dressing, and in the beginning of our relationship, she would leave her Ranch dressing plates in the sink to be washed. This was before we had a dishwasher, and the two of us would pile the dishes in the sink till one of us caved and washed them. During this quarantine though, the amount of ketchup consumed drove me up the walls. I was saving packets from food delivery before I was buying another economy-size bottle. It's ridiculous now that I think about it, but the more you know yourself, I guess the better?

## No Birthday Sex?

*"Day 55...*

*Rowan wakes up at 6:15am... "Dad I have something in my tummy button."*

*I take a look... he has a tick... in his belly button... my wife hates bugs... and she's not a morning person... and it's Mother's Day... I get her tweezers out... because the tick tornado I bought can't reach it... tug and out it comes... Rowan didn't even flinch, which after his drama-filled appendix rupture or as it turns out trampoline-excessive use diagnosis, this would have been the time to have a professional do it... and this is the time he's fine...*

*I called my mother at 7:30am... I am positive I will be the first of my siblings to wish her a happy Mother's Day... I will definitely beat my brother to it, because he probably doesn't know it's Mother's Day... but my sister is the best child of all of us, so to beat her is bragging rights... my mother was happy to hear from me... she just got off the phone with my sister... 7am on a Sunday and she already called... some people are just over-achievers...*

*My wife loves breakfast and I love cheese and sausage charcuterie boards... so this morning I made a pancake charcuterie board... the fact that I made a pound of bacon and sausage each followed by a dozen pancakes and mounds of sugary toppings didn't bother her... because it was her day... and the sugar intake of my 7-year-old falls on me today... I didn't think it through...*

*I sent my mother and mother-in-law cookies in the mail... I know they will appreciate them... 2 dozen each... go big or go home...*

*Happy Mother' Day to all you Mothers."*

*"Day 56...*

*I can't pinpoint the age, when your child starts to argue with you, but I can say that at age 7, they start to present arguments with logic, even if the logic is off...*

*Rowan wanted to ride his bike... I told him to put on a sweatshirt... he argued that the sun is out, and he would not need one... I told him it's cold... he said it's not... this continued until my wife, overhearing the argument asked Rowan to come over, and proceeded to put her cold hands under his shirt against his skin... he put on a sweatshirt shortly after... my wife is a genius...*

*I went to the pub today... to get beer inventory with a distributor for credit to the kegs that will need to be replaced upon our re-opening... I still really miss what I do, even after all the days of sweatpants and cookies...*

*When I came home, Rowan was using the bathroom... when he was finished, he exited the bathroom proudly announcing he remembered to turn the fan on and use the "not-poop smelling" spray... I asked if he washed his hands... he hesitated to answer but then saw my wife... he went back in and washed his hands... my wife is a boss...*

*I ate low-carb bread today... but then I also ate 3 cookies on my way to the pub... I have never asked the cookie lady the carb count on her cookies, so I am not going to count those carbs..."*

*"Day 57...*

*It is good to know that if you lose your lawn tractor key, a locksmith has all the brands on hand to replace them... I know this because "we" lost the key... I have never been allowed to mow the lawn in over 15 years because I ran over "decorative grass", and my punishment was never being allowed to mow again... I know, this is the best punishment ever... but "we" lost the key...*

*My wife let Rowan use her foot bath last night... he has used it 4 times today... and now his action figures are using it as a pool...*

*"We" found the key... it was on my wife's nightstand on her side of the bed... I found it, but it's a team effort...*

*Rowan is doing his spelling homework... and using Alexa to tell him how to spell words... I'm sort of proud that he thought to do this, but I know when my wife comes in from mowing the lawn, I am sure she will not be happy I let him do it... so after the 2nd word, I told him he couldn't do it anymore...*

*I had to go get gas for the mower... "We" apparently ran out...*

*Rowan asked me how to spell "eight" ... but it was "ate" ... he told me if I had let him use Alexa, this wouldn't have happened...*

*I started attempting to get beer never tapped in Kalamazoo before for our anniversary party today... Tuesdays are beer delivery days normally....*

*God, I miss it..."*

*"Day 58...*

*I have never ordered anything from Groupon that I need, or that lasts more than a couple uses... with that said... if someone else could make a Star Wars ice cube molds that resemble the Death Star, an abdomen belt that gives you a six-pack as advertised, or iPhone cords that work for the same low price, I would greatly appreciate it...*

*Rowan has started leaning on the netting of the trampoline, no matter how many times he has been asked not to... it now has a small hole... the part of me that wants to see the accident bound to happened does not outweigh the fatherly instinct that I must replace it... I am becoming an adult, and how dare my son make me do that!...*

*My wife asked me to build her a trellis for her garden... honestly, if we were an HGTV show I would watch us, because if I don't get hurt doing the construction, the number of times my wife speaks to me like I'm an idiot is likely to happen more than a person can count every 20-minute episode... If you turned it into a drinking game, you'd die...*

*We started watching "Star Wars, Episode 2: Attack of the Clones" ... the worst Star Wars movie ever made... not up for debate... it's a fact... Happy Wednesday."*

My wife and I never had a talk of becoming parents outside of my eldest son. Angela never brought up a biological need for her own child, and I am not sure if it was because she didn't want to with me, or if she didn't want to for herself. I am not sure if the stress of being a stepparent was a lot or seeing how I raise my son as his biological father wasn't good in her eyes, or if she even thought that at all. I don't know if she didn't want children because she was raised in a house of 5 kids, and having personal space was relaxing. I am an analytical individual, which is a nice way of saying I overthink, cause myself anxiety, and my insecurities get the best of me.

When I hurt my right knee playing soccer and thought that I may need to see a doctor for it, I was surprised it was more than just a sports injury.

I had an ultrasound and series of X-Rays done, and what was found was a Giant Cell Tumor. It sounds worse than it is. From what I gather, it is a benign tumor that can grow to the size of a softball and eats away at bone. I had 3 previous surgeries for this and each one left a trace of tumor that grew back to a concerning density, annually. The final time, upon its return, the Surgeon suggested I consider a clinical drug trial. I don't recall the name of the drug, my wife paid attention more than I did, but it was used to treat patients with Osteoporosis. The Doctors had found that it transformed the tumor cells into bone over time. I had to take calcium supplements and get a shot in my stomach every month as well as x-rays to my jaw and chest because they found complications with some patients affecting the lungs and jawbone. It was during this meeting that they told us that we could not have children while I was on this trial, because they weren't sure how it would affect my sperm (If it did at all).

My wife paused upon this news. I wasn't sure what she was contemplating. Then she looked up from her daze, and said,

"What?"

"We can't have sex. No sex?"

The poor Doctor tried to remain positive,

"Not unprotected."

Angela with anxiety,

"Tomorrow's my birthday. No birthday sex?"

I was kind of shocked by this question. I didn't realize how important "Birthday Sex" was. Looking at my wife, and studying her face, this was a new emotion.

"Doctor, can you give us a minute?"

I believe the Doctor was relieved to hear the question and made her way out of the room.

Ultimately, it was decided we would need a month or so to decide what was best for us. Sometime in January of 2012, and my wife could probably pinpoint the moment, she was pregnant with Rowan.

Angela tells the story to our son that she didn't know she needed him until she was told she couldn't have him. I'll take that explanation any day of the week, because it means I was always part of the equation for us. No matter how many years, and how much time you spend with another person, it's great never to take for granted what they mean to you. My mother was the definition of the word, "nurturer", and I hope to help instill the same relationship for my sons to have with my wife. Mother's Day takes new meaning here, because we are the parents now, and it is a celebration of Angela for all she does to nurture our sons.

I always knew my wife was for me, from the minute I held her hand for the first time. I remember hoping I was a good enough kisser, because kissing is my wife's favorite. I remember meeting her father. Her mother. Her brothers and sister. These people that are my family now. If someday when I die, and I am graced with God's presence, I will thank him for steering me to my wife, and her to me.

## Cancel Culture in the Restaurant Industry

*"Day 59...*

*Rowan likes "Attack of the Clones" better than "A New Hope", and he doesn't understand sarcasm, so I can't even make a joke about grounding him...*

*I am grouchy about lights being left on in rooms not being used, which I don't normally get mad about, due to the relation it brings to being a "Dad", although I have left my tv and computer on for hours without using them. My gutters are not working efficiently, because the heavy rainstorm has a waterfall forming in the corners of each end of the house. I am tending to a fireplace fire that I didn't use a starter log to start and now I must constantly check to make sure it isn't going out... this quarantine is turning me into a grumpy old man...*

*My wife has been up and productive since 6am... she is exercising in our basement... my major accomplishment for the day has been counting the number of Hipster Chipster cookies I finished in a little over 3 weeks... there are 4 remaining in the freezer... 92 have been consumed...*

*I have been reading the "Tales of a 4th Grade Nothing" series to my 7-year-old because it was my favorite book series when I was his age... it holds up, but the kids are very disrespectful in it... crazy how your opinion changes when your role in life is different...*

*It's Thursday for those that need the reminder..."*

*"Day 60...*

*I just saw a post asking for recommendations for best socks for running... I have a recommendation, but I can't imagine having me as your source is going to be taken seriously...*

*My cat has been treating life like he's on a Vegas-bender and thinks sleep won't matter during this weather... he escaped last night at 3:30am while I was taking the dog out during the Thunderstorm... I waited for him to come home, which I thought would be soon because of the weather... 90 minutes later, he casually strolled back on the deck...*

*I went back to bed at 4:30am... the cat knocked on the door with his paws at 5am... till he was let out again... Rowan woke up at 6am...*

*My wife heard nothing... she didn't even know it stormed last night... she woke up with energy and positivity, read the Bible with Rowan, and planned for us to go mushroom hunting... I ate an espresso cookie... there are only 3 left...*

*I saw breaded avocado slices at the store, so I bought some... avocados are best eaten cold or at room temperature and not breaded or fried, which is weird, because everything tastes better with breading and deep fried...*

*I know its Friday afternoon, and I don't remember the last time I took a nap, but Rowan wants to watch "Revenge of the Sith", so now is the perfect time...*

*2 months in... I never would have believed you if you told me this lockdown would last this long..."*

*"Day 61…*

*My wife found soil for her garden in the woods behind our house… she made me touch it… she made our neighbors touch it… everyone seemed excited… they went back to the woods to gather more soil together… I might be losing my mind, but it's dirt… my excitement has been contained…*

*I am officially out of the cookies I ordered from the cookie lady… There are Oreos here though…*

*The weather today was nice enough to wear shorts… little by little, I miss sweatpants…*

*My Crowler machine shipped today, but the cookie dough I ordered was postponed… my wife thinks we are out of sugar and is unaware of this order and it's a lot… because variety is the spice of life…"*

*"Day 62…*

*Went to bed at midnight… 2am… my dog has to go out and my wife wakes me saying, "she has to go out, don't let her jump down." The cat sneaks out with the dog… 4am… the cat gets into a fight with another animal outside of our window… jumping out of bed as fast as I can, my wife asks, "what's wrong?" the cat comes in and avoids me… 6am… my 7-year-old wakes me for the day… 9am… my wife wakes up and has no recollection of any of it…*

*We had 4 packs of Oreos this morning… or so I thought… it appears that each have been opened with less than 3 remaining in each… my wife and 7-year-old had the rest after church…*

*I took a shower to help wake me up... it didn't work... so I made tacos...*

*The dog stole my wife's last Oreo...*

*Rowan wants to play LEGO Avengers for the Xbox... we have finished 99% of the game and can't get the last mission done because of a glitch... there is absolutely no point to play because we can't do anything else... it's silly for me to say, but it makes me feel unproductive... Me!*

*Sunday... I am pretty excited because I have to work tomorrow at getting the pub ready for a reopen... almost there..."*

*"Day 63...*

*I woke up knowing I had to go to work, and excited is not the proper word to describe my emotion... Rowan woke up and saw that it was still rainy out and was determined not to let it get him down... He said, "well at least it's not snowing." If it had been snowing, he would have gotten a sled out... I must admire his positive approach to the world though...*

*Our neighbors yard sometimes floods to what appears to be a mini lake... it is not uncommon to see ducks swimming in their backyard from time to time... what you don't see? 7-year-old children laying down in the middle of it to see how deep it is, fully clothed, and disappointed that he can't swim in it due to its lack of depth... when my wife came home from running errands, she saw a shirtless, sockless boy on the trampoline... jumping in the rain... I went to work...*

*My beer reps came and did an inventory count... replacements coming as soon as we get the green light to re-open... It was eerie seeing people who I worked so closely with on a week-to-week basis for the first time in 2 months after 19 years of routine...*

*I got home to my son finding a fallen bird's nest, and the sentence, "I saved that baby birds life" at least 100 times... he asked me to compliment him on the job he did... he's 7... and is asking for acknowledgement to his heroics...*

*Monday... I still have never started the week with a workout, but I have 2 more Mondays to go... I think..."*

What was supposed to be 2 weeks, had expanded to over 2 months. I had not spoken to any of my suppliers or vendors in that time. The restaurant industry was hard before the pandemic but highlighted so much more when we had been through it now. A lot of places in town lost their staff to other occupations, particularly "medicinal" shops. If you are a cook at any restaurant, and if you are any good, you definitely are an expert on cannabis. It comes with the brochure for "How to be a line cook."

Some places just closed, because it was uncertain how we would survive such a layoff when a lot of independent restaurants live paycheck to paycheck. Or they were close to retirement, and now seemed as good a time as any. All of us were so tired.

Thick skin is something you must grow as a restaurant owner, especially in the days of cancel culture. I have seen a lot. From a brewery opened by two Peace Corp. activists who were accused of racism, to a full-fledged Neo-Nazi posting pics of himself at rallies. The Nazi guy deserved to be shut down. He was preaching hate. The Peace Corp. guys, not so much. They handled an accusation of racism poorly, sticking to their belief that they were for peace and love amongst all people but not seeing what they were saying sounded sketchy. They wound up apologizing and seeking education on what they did wrong.

At the end of the day, we all learn something about what offends someone and what you should do better at. I am not perfect, and no one else is either. I will give someone the benefit of the doubt though, if by all accounts, they were just trying to be a good person. The world needs more good people.

Here I was though, in my pub for the first time in a long-time doing work with a beer distributor. We all shared our pandemic stories and small talk.

"What'd you do to pass time?"

"I had "it", but my wife never did."

"My wife had "it", but I never did."

"We both thought we had "it" because we were sick, and then tested negative. Then we felt better and tested positive."

"Did you really eat that many cookies?"

This was also the first time I had spoken to someone outside of my immediate surroundings that told me they read my "Pandemic Diary", and it helped them get through. It became a thing. As we began to open, I would run in to more and more people who said the same. I was blown away, because I was just making these daily posts for me. I had no idea others would love it so much. Some even asked me to have them published. That's why I am writing this today.

We hadn't been given a solid answer as to when the lockdown would be over, or what it would look like when it was lifted. We all had a feeling it was soon, and that within the next couple of weeks, we would be back. If you stop doing something routine, it amazes me how tiring trying to get back to it is. I worked 8 hours that day cleaning, doing inventory, calling staff to see who was coming back, deciding on hours of operation. I was so exhausted when I got home that I went to sleep almost immediately after dinner. It was only 8 hours! Crazy how life comes at you sometimes.

## The Haircut

*"Day 64...*

*Having a conversation with my 7-year-old where I exclaim, "Mom is not my boss" is a slippery slope... first, he looks at me confused as if I don't know that she's my boss... further, I say it enough to where I start to wonder, "Is she my boss?". Lastly, I say it quietly, so she doesn't hear me, which is proof enough, I have a boss...*

*Better Made Salt & Vinegar Potato Chips are the saltiest, vinegar-iest of all salt and vinegar chips...*

*Telling a 7-year-old, "Don't hit anybody with that stick.", guarantees somebody is getting hit with a stick...*

*Flavor combinations can be disappointing or surprisingly splendid... I love cinnamon... I love Coca-Cola... I do not love Cinnamon Coca-Cola...*

*It appears the activity to pass time we do most now is hunt for mushrooms... My wife has no idea the amount of anxiety it creates for me when I think I have found something and she makes me wait in one place till she gets to me, which is always longer than necessary... people with ADHD, I know you understand this..."*

*"Day 65...*

*My wife lives vicariously through other people... her sister is buying a new house and my wife spends loads of time looking at houses for sale in her sister's area... but my wife doesn't want to move...*

*My wife's friends just announced she was pregnant with a 5th child, and my wife is so happy for her... but my wife doesn't want another baby...*

*It's refreshing to see someone who is so supportive of others instead of pulling them down... it's even better that I married such a person...*

*My beer distributor gave me a zero carb/zero sugar energy drink... it's not for me... the Red Bull lady gave me a watermelon Red Bull... It's not for me either...*

*My cookie dough delivery is on back order... this is terrible news...*

*Not having gotten a real haircut in 2 months has me thinking I look alright with a lot of hair...*

*It's Wednesday, and that's the day I usually get a haircut..."*

*"Day 66...*

*My 7-year-old woke me up to watch "Return of the Jedi" at 6:15am... while situating myself on the couch to go back to sleep, he sits next to me, hugs me, and whispers, "Dad, I'm going to fart on you" ... Apparently, this is the "go to" threat if I try and sleep during the movie...*

*I ate a fish sandwich from Culver's for lunch... it doesn't make any sense why I would crave it, because I hate fish, but it was delicious... and I wish I had gotten another... maybe my wife's friend being pregnant has me living vicariously through her too...*

*Discover Kalamazoo Inc. reached out to me today to join a "Comeback Marketing Task Force"... I am assuming none of executive members are friends with me on Facebook, because this quarantine diary isn't a ringing endorsement of the value I bring to the table...*

*I have a King-size Kit Kat I bought for making s'mores last week that my entire family is unaware of... the problem is, I am sure they make King-size candy bars for multiple snack times but all I see is the buffet option of a Kit Kat bar and with buffets probably becoming a thing of the past, I should probably celebrate what once was... it's the honorable thing to do...*

*Gatherings of 10 or less are ok right now... so I am going to build a fire in my backyard and hope others will see, bring a chair, and sit around watching it burn with me...*

*Happy Thursday."*

*"Day 67...*

*My son woke up at 5:47am... after staying up till 11pm last night... my wife made him go back to bed... in my spot... I was sent to the bean bag, but Rowan slept till 10:45am... that's a win...*

*My wife started making breakfast, but being 11am now, it was brunch... she was singing, "Tootsie Roll", but changed the lyrics to "Brunch, baby, Brunch" ...*

*Rowan has daily vitamins my wife picked up from the Health Food Center... thy are zoo-shaped animals... this morning I heard him complain, "Ugh, it's always an Elephant" ... he ate it anyway...*

*I just realized my favorite active/workout shirt is a White Castle T-shirt... I didn't work out... but I'm going to order lunch now...*

*I just got an email that my cookie dough has shipped...*

*My wife is planting vegetables in our garden... she and the neighbor are discussing determinate and indeterminate plants... I made a fruit wreath in animal crossing today for my door... it's almost the same thing... No one ever knocks on my door in the game... I think the wreath deters people... it must be determinate...*

*Happy Friday."*

Now that we had been given the greenlight to gather in groups of 10 or more, people were feeling more comfortable to make plans for visits with each other. My wife is an active church member, participating in Bible study groups, and leading children's classes. I am not as invested in organized religion, and to my wife's credit, she has not forced it on me. I can feel her disappointment at times when she goes to church and I don't, but there are occasions when I do go, but that's another story.

In this instance, a group of ladies were coming over on a Friday afternoon to have coffee and Bible talk. I felt this was as good a time as any to visit the barber shop, since I hadn't been in over 2 months, and they were finally able to re-open. I like barbershops, not hair stylist places. I grew up going with my grandfather to place with 6 barbers who chain smoked, complained about the government, their wives, their mortgage, their health, etc. It was an education into the late 70's/early 80's male mentality. These guys were visibly miserable people, and as a 4–6-year-old, it was highly entertaining.

I also choose my barbershop based on distance from my home. The closer the better. I have never had 1 barber I was sold on going to. Until we moved to Portage. Angela and I took Rowan to get a haircut at one of the franchised barbershops. They did a nice job on kid's haircuts, they weren't very pricey, and really, with little kids you can always just buzz cut their hair if it looks uneven. While we were there, my "people watching" senses kicked in. There was a new lady hair stylist, who was having trouble getting anyone to let her cut their hair. Most people had their chosen person. I was close to needing a haircut anyway, and asked her,

"Do you think you have time to cut mine?"

She looked up from her chair and with a smile, said,

"Yes!"

I got my haircut, and it was simple and easy, and even, and manageable. Her name was Amber, and I went to get my haircut from Amber for a better part of 3 years, over many of the places she wound up working, because she didn't stay at the original barbershop I met her at for very long.

She was my first "hair stylist" that I would go to see on a regular basis. As time would have it, Amber gave me a call earlier in the week to let me know that she had returned to the place I first met her.

"Really?", I asked.

"They needed people, and I need a job after not cutting hair for 2 months, so it fits.", she said.

I told her I would be in soon, but didn't make an appointment, because I never know when I will have time. It's a walk-in kind of place, and those work best for me. Amber was the kind of stylist who worked every day, so when I would go in, if I saw her, I just waited. If she wasn't there, I would leave. I had to be out of the house for Bible time, so this seemed like as good a time as any.

I took Rowan with me, since it was his barbershop anyway, and he could get his haircut too. We went in, and I set Rowan up to get his haircut, and then asked,

"I'm here to see Amber?"

The receptionist behind the counter sadly told me,

"Oh, Amber is off, she has COVID, she won't be back for a couple of weeks."

I said, "Ok", and went to sit back down and wait for Rowan to get his haircut done, but this lady was inquisitive,

"Do you want me to do it?"

"I have been going to Amber for a while, I'll just wait.", I said.

She doubled down,

"I can do it, what do you usually get?"

At this moment, I could have said a couple of things. I could have said, "No, I'll wait to see Amber" or I could have said, "Just a number 2 on the sides faded into finger length on the top (barber lingo)." Either of those things would have been acceptable. That's not what I did.

"Amber had mentioned doing an undercut next time I was in, but I have never had that and was going to let her try it out, but I think I will just go back to my usual."

This is me in a nutshell. I get nervous talking to people about things I am not well-versed in, and then I talk more than I should. Next thing you know, I have put myself in a place I can't get out of. This was about to be the case.

"I have done thousands of undercuts.", she said.

I didn't want to get this haircut, but I needed one, and she did double-down, so she was confident in her ability. I said,

"Ok".

There was a tv on, and I paid attention to what was playing on Sportscenter more than what was happening to my hair, but there seemed to be a lot of time and care being taken into my undercut. The electric razor cuts were slow, and meticulous. This was giving me confidence that maybe this was going to work out. About 20 minutes in, this nice barber lady turned me towards the mirror to ask me what I thought. She had shaved the right side of my head to almost bald. The other side was completely full, and the top was still very long. It looked like we were halfway done, so I said,

"It looks good so far."

She was in the motion of taking my apron off, when I finished this sentence, so she paused.

"It's done.", she said.

I looked panicked but calmly I asked, "What about the other side?"

At this point my hair looked like "Kate Plus 8" and that I was a "Karen" about to ask for a manager.

She snapped the apron back on, and said,

"Ok, so you want it shaved all around and the top to cover?"

"I guess so?", I had no idea.

The razor turned back on, but this time, the slow, methodical strokes had been replaced with rushed, fast paced sweeps back and forth, and I could feel that we are now in the "winging it" stage of this haircut. I tried to pay attention to Sportscenter, but my eyes kept drifting to the mirror. Both sides of my head are now close to bald, but the fade into the top was non-existent, and closer and closer to the top of my head was being shaved. I realized this was not working, so I calmly said,

"Stop. We are going to just call it good."

She looked at me and asked,

"Well, what are you going to do?"

I looked at the mirror. My head looked like the pineapple SpongeBob lives in under the sea.

"I'm going to go home and shave it."

She looked at me and said,

"I can do that."

"No, I got it. This is my fault, I didn't know what I wanted, and I am going to chalk this up to a learning experience.", I said.

I paid her. I tipped well. I am certain others may argue that I shouldn't have but arguing this with my current haircut would have been fitting, and I don't need to be filmed by a stranger and made famous on the internet. It would have been hilarious though.

Rowan and I got in the car. Rowan looked at me, and said,

"I really like my haircut, Dad. I don't really like yours."

I looked in the mirror, looked at my son, and said,

"Your mother is going to kill me."

We got home and Rowan ran inside. I followed slowly behind. My wife was in the living room with her group of church ladies, and I hear her put on the "We have guests" voice as she says,

"Oh, my handsome boy!"

Rowan, without missing a beat, smiling from ear to ear,

"Yeah, I know, you should see Dad."

I waited in the kitchen. There was no way I was going to the living room yet. I like to make an entrance, but I feel my wife should be the first to see this mess.

I hear her walking, not really prepared for what she is about to see, and she makes eye contact with me.

Stunned, she pauses and says,

"Oh Fuck."

"MOM!",

Rowan said, knowing we had members of the church over and this word is frowned upon.

She looks at me again,

"Ted. Fuck."

"MOM!",

again, from Rowan.

"ROWAN!,

Angela escalated her voice, but realizes there is company over and snaps out of it, so she whispers to me,

"Fuck".

The ladies in the other room can't control their curiosity, so they come around the corner, and each of them, trying to be nice, say nothing, but I can feel the combustible laughter they are unsuccessfully controlling as they walk back into the living room.

"Relax, we have electric clippers, I'm going to shave it.",

I assured my wife.

I went to find them. We bought these clippers 20 years ago when we moved into our first apartment. I used to shave my head to a light buzz, because it was cheaper, and I hadn't found a barber yet. I hadn't used them in at least 18 years. They needed to be lubricated and made the most horrendously loud sound when I turned them on. As I turned them on, I hear my wife shout,

"TED! STOP!"

I opened the bathroom door, to see Angela on the phone, in front of her church friends, talking to someone,

"Yes, my husband did a thing, I need you to fix it."

She paused before she continued talking,

"No, now. ASAP!"

Another pause from the phone as she listens to their answer. She thanks them and hangs up, turns to me,

"You need to go downtown; I called a place that my stylist recommended for you.",

She hands me a hat.

"Put this on and don't take it off till you get there."

I can see the relief that a professional is going to fix this in her eyes, but the cheap side of me is taking over.

"I already paid for this; I don't want to pay for 2 haircuts."

"YOU PAID?!",

Angela shouted.

"Well, yeah, I didn't give good instructions...", I said before being interrupted.

"Just go. Ask for Colby",

my wife said.

I get downtown to a Men's clothing/barbershop combo place. Very hipster-ish, and not really my style, as I stick out like a sore thumb in my sweatpants and Detroit Lions shirt and hat.

"I'm here to see Colby?", I asked.

Leading me to the back of the shop are two barber's chairs. It's the most out of place Barber shop I had seen, but this seems to be the new concept of hair, and I am showing my age.

This good-looking well-groomed kid dressed in a black apron and gloves, looking like "Dexter" preparing to dismember a body is waiting for me. If I had to describe the word "Cool", this young man is the definition.

"Let's see it.",

are the first words that he says to me. I reluctantly take my hat off, only to hear this reaction,

"Holy shit! Where did you go?",

he asked.

In my head, I feel like he doesn't know the whole story and needs to before I tell him, but as I start to say that it isn't the point of where I went, it's the circumstances, he stops me,

"Where did you go?"

I told him. He throws his hands to the side,

"That's why."

He says as he leads me to sit in the chair and study the mess on my head.

I remember the next part so clearly, as it felt as if this were life or death, but Colby kneels in front of me, starts tapping his hand on my knee, and says,

"Ok, I am going to give it to you straight, I don't know if I can fix this. I am going to try. It's not going to be my best work, but I think you will be able to leave here with hair on your head, and without a hat on."

This was the funniest thing he could have said to me, and I was excited that I had this story to eventually tell when it was all over. The kneeling down and talking to me like I was a kindergartner was fantastic. It may have been insulting to some, but really, I was at his mercy to help me, and he could have said whatever he wanted.

Colby worked slowly and with such precision. He took this horrible haircut and fixed it to a presentable Hipster style that wasn't fitting of me, but it was growing on me.

He often said while working,

"Man, did she do you dirty."

I left without a hat on, made it home to my wife and son who had said goodbye to the Bible group sometime while I was gone. Angela came into the kitchen as I entered from the garage and a sigh of relief came over her.

I have gone to Colby ever since. He has switched to many different shops, and they are all farther than I normally would go, and I have to make an appointment each time rather than walk-in, but the man is a Master of his craft. I didn't check on Amber to see if she was ok or explain to her that I switched to a new Barber. I never heard from her again, so either her co-worker filled her in, or she really isn't ok. I have come to this realization as I write this. Amber, if you're reading this, no hard feelings, and I hope you're ok?

## Monster Rehab, you owe me some swag!

*"Day 68...*

*I got an email from a waterpark in Wisconsin advertising $20 room rates with free water park passes... this is usually $250 a night... it made me think... somebody is going to market waterproof face masks... I'm still not going...*

*I have moved on from Oreos to making s'mores every night... a bonfire without them is like going to the movies and not getting popcorn...*

*I am wearing a tie dye shirt today... it was inspired by my character in Animal Crossing owning one now... It's like I'm an avatar from the game...*

*I don't know if my hair looks good to other people... I think it does... but no one is here to judge it... with this shirt on, the focus probably wouldn't be on my hair...*

*It's always nice when the warmest day of the week is on a Saturday..."*

*"Day 69 (Nice)...*

*One of the neighbors who supplied Oreos invited us to use their pool... so I brought a lot of Oreos... because you shouldn't come over empty handed...*

*I had to convince people at their small gathering that the song Pinball Wizard has the lyrics, "Deaf, Dumb, and Blind Kid" ... in the context that sounds worse than it's meant to be...*

*Rowan's diet today consists of sneaking Oreos... my wife was distracted... and I'm not a sell-out... there's a lesson to be learned here...*

*My cat went outside and decided it was too hot to stay out... he gave me a dirty look... he is certain I control the weather...*

*It doesn't feel like a Sunday..."*

*"Day 70...*

*If bread and sugar were the healthiest foods for you, I would be a celebrity Cross-fit trainer...*

*My 7-year-old swam and jumped on a trampoline for nearly 6 hours yesterday... he woke up sore at midnight and woke my wife up... because "Mom knows how to fix sore arms" ...*

*My wife needed more dirt from the holy grail of dirt piles in our back woods... so I volunteered to get it on our tractor... Rowan goes rock hunting while I do this... he found 20 "crystal rocks that will sell for $300 each" ... I don't know how to tell him that they are worthless, but I am trying to negotiate a cheaper price to show him how bartering works... he thinks a quarter is too cheap...*

*I was at the pub today... I now have a game plan in place for when we re-open our doors as it goes for the dining room layout... I can't wait to hear that kitchen ticket machine again...*

*I haven't dreamt of it in a while..."*

*"Day 71...*

*I worked all day at the pub... I set up my Crowler machine... a few of my staff members came in and cleaned... I posted that we are going to open on Friday and Saturday for curbside pickup from 4pm-8pm each day... 3 hours after the post, 14,000 people have viewed it... I am overwhelmed and truly humbled...*

*I usually try to make this daily post a light, semi-humorous rant about my family... with all that is going on in social media, I would rather be on the lighter side of things... but today's post isn't very funny, just full of appreciation...*

*Being gone all day, I was greeted by my 7-year-old who showed me a scroll he made at school counting to 1600... handwritten... I am exhausted looking at it...*

*Dear, God... I have a good life...*

*Happy Tuesday..."*

At this time of life, I was trying to get back into the groove of working long hours, but my energy levels had decreased so drastically. Each day increased more and more, but I hate waiting for results. This has caused many bad habits over the years, and one of those is my reliance on energy drinks.

I was never much of a Red Bull guy. They are fine, and they work, but they very much have that sweet tart flavor to them, and it takes me a minute to get past that. However, if I find a drink I love, I drink it till the wheels fall off. Before I met Angela, I was obsessed with Coca-Cola. I worked at

Target while I was in college, and got an employee discount, so when 12 packs would go on sale for $1.99, I would buy a half pallet and store it in my shared rental home. My room was wall-to-wall with cases of it. That changed when I had my one and only kidney stone. I don't know what it is like to give birth to a child, but the fact that it hurts more than a kidney stone, I have nothing but respect for my wife and mother. I want to apologize to both of you for having something to do with this sort of pain.

When the pub opened, I was hooked on a drink called "Function Light Weight". It wasn't carbonated, it was a light flavored juice-like pomegranate mango. I lost 12 lbs. just consuming this drink, so it had benefits on top of flavor. Then I went in for my knee surgeries and was asked to stop doing all my daily routines, so I never went back to it. I was drinking a lot of water from that point on, but then one day, I was working at the pub, and was so thirsty. I remembered that one of my reps brought in sample cans of Monster Rehab Lemonade Iced Tea. I had left it in the cooler for some time, and it was cold, but I didn't like energy drinks much. I tried it anyway. It wasn't carbonated and didn't taste at all like an energy drink should. It was 25 calories per can! SOLD! I was now officially a Monster Rehab guy. They had flavors too. I wound up hooked on Pink Lemonade and bought cases and cases. There was a crazy church lady video someone shared with me about how Monster was the mark of the devil. So stupid that the Pepsi Co. was run by Satan, who knew?

Then Monster discontinued my favorite Pink Lemonade flavor, so I bought all the remaining cases I could find in

West Michigan and drank it for 6 months past its availability. I then boycotted Monster because they took my flavor away. That, and they had a loyalty program where you send in can caps from what you purchased and they would send you stuff like sleeping bags, and calendars, a mountain bike, or cutlery. I could get everything in the entire catalog, twice. I sent them in, and they never sent me a thing.

So back to water it was, until this little Seltzer water company came into town, called Bubbl'r. These drinks were SUPER carbonated, which really wasn't my thing, but for whatever reason, I fell in love with them. So much so, that I personally was the #3 account with the distributor behind Meijer and Walmart. Not Shakespeare's as the #3 account. Just Ted Vadella. Go big or go home. They sent me a Bubbl'r refrigerator for my support. I didn't even have to send in a can cap. Suck it, Monster!

I say that, but then, something happened. Monster came out with a Strawberry Lemonade Rehab. I am back on the Monster train.

I rarely sleep, and the argument could be made that I have too many energy drinks, but really, my focus is better, my creativity is better, and I am on top of my game with my improv abilities. Monster, you are something.

## The Unnamed Door Guy

*"Day 72...*

*Today is supposed to be the cookie dough delivery day... I received an email from the cookie dough people saying that "some" orders are not going to be the highest quality and I can ask for a refund... I haven't received it yet... but with an email like that, my wife said it's a sign that I don't need it... I say that it's a sign that I now have a 20% off coupon...*

*When I find something comfortable to wear, I usually buy the exact same thing in a different color... I own 3 different colored jogging shorts of the same style... they have never been used for their exact purpose...*

*My son told me today that my wife gave him a ton of animal crackers... now he's selling my wife out... I want to tell him what a mistake he has made, but guess he's got to learn the hard way...*

*My Crowler machine came on a brand-new fresh pallet... I brought it home for my wife for her garden... she was so happy... It's like a "get out of jail, free" card... now I just have to figure out when to cash it in today...*

*Happy Wednesday..."*

*"Day 73... THE LAST DAY!*

*Today, I have done nothing but take pre-orders for carry-out nachos, and there are hundreds of them! I am humbled, thrilled, overwhelmed, and tearfully happy...*

*I will miss all the time each day I have spent eating Oreos, sneaking more snacks in from my wife, and watching each minute of the day with my 7-year-old, but there is this light, and the tunnel is ending...*

*I'm back! Back to doing what I love, and with the people I love doing it with every day...*

*I hope my wife will miss these posts... she made each of them special...*

*Thank you, friends, for reading them... for reaching out and letting me know they were important to your days...*

*Happy Thursday...*

*My cup is so full..."*

This was the end of the first restaurant lock down. It was mid-June. We were now able to open our doors to 50 people, with tables spread 6 feet apart, and parties no more than 6 at a table. You had to wear a mask from the front door till you were seated at your table and then you could take your mask off. Our capacity at the pub was 401 people, and when the patio was open, our occupancy shifted to 525 people. We could only operate with 50 people. After the first two weeks, we were allowed to operate with 100 people, and then further in it changed to

200 people. It never got back to full capacity between June and November, when they shut us down a second time.

It didn't really matter, because the consumer was still very cautious and downtown Kalamazoo was a shell of its former self in our industry. The surrounding restaurants were either closed permanently, not able to reopen due to staffing shortages, or extremely strict with their occupancy policies.

We were busier than most, and Scott and I can't say enough how thankful we were to the many people who supported us and continue to support us. We had heard of people refusing to wear masks at places or fighting the staff over the State mandated rulings. It rarely happened to us, and when it did, it was from someone who had never been to our place before. A large portion of our staff came back to work for us, even though they were still allowed to collect the massive unemployment increase to stay home. We only had 1 door staff member who claimed to be afraid, called us irresponsible for opening, and was upset that he may lose out on the extra money by refusing to come to work. We never made anyone return to work "Or else". When the unnamed door guy found out we didn't force him, that he could stay home and continue to collect his unemployment, he was thrilled. This same door staff member joined a co-ed soccer team, playing in close quarters with strangers, and had the nerve to come into the pub for dinner on a Saturday night, but wouldn't work in the same place. He is a garbage human being who uses social agendas to expand his presence. "Look at me, I care" but also makes it about himself.

Once, we had a group, called the "Proud Boys" come into the pub. This was before they made National headlines as a hate group and had little notoriety. They dress in what appears to be University of Michigan colors, which is ironic, because they came in only to watch Michigan games. They did this for 3 weeks, only on Saturdays, keeping to themselves in the back corner, and not being a presence of any kind. We learned of them from this unnamed door guy. He let them in on a busy Saturday night, then proceeded to find a manager to tell them who they were and that he was walking out if we didn't throw them out, immediately.

He let them in!

My manager on duty called me and asked what we should do. I had never heard of them. I looked them up, and if you have never done this, they seem like a fraternity joke. It just didn't seem real. We had 150 people in the pub this day, and now 30 Proud Boys. With 3 door staff members. Asking them to leave seemed like we were putting the crowd we had in danger and didn't feel the proper authorities would do anything unless given reason. Thankfully, they tried to "recruit" someone, and when they were asked not to do so by one of our servers, they verbally attacked her, so we asked them to leave, and they did, without physicality. We immediately addressed the staff and made a social media post about these "proud boys" so that we could warn our surrounding neighbors of their existence and potential patronage. From my experience, Kalamazoo doesn't let hate breed here. I am proud to say that, and even happier to say that the Proud Boys are not welcome in our establishment.

The unnamed door guy had left before the Proud Boys were asked to leave. Then returned the next day and apologized and asked to work again. We gave him the benefit of doubt and told him that the next time he had information that we didn't he should ask for a manager so we can head it off at the door, rather than put a crowd of people in danger. I didn't realize at that moment he was trying to make himself a hero by making a scene in front of an unsuspecting crowd. It was about him, not the cause.

He is the reason I learned the definition of "gaslighting", lying with ease and not recognizing this in their own behavior. Denying they said something that you clearly heard them say. Manipulating someone into questioning their own sanity. I really have spent more time on him than he deserves but the lessons I have learned about how I don't want to be when supporting causes that need support, I owe to him.

He returned to work when the pandemic payouts were stopped, only to get a job within his field and leave shortly after. I congratulated him and thanked him for his time. He took the time to tell us he didn't respect us or who we employed and even went further to say our pay rate was inappropriate for having the biggest bar in Kalamazoo.

It's funny how restaurant wages are attacked often from people who have not had to pay to operate them. There is grey area here. I don't know what it costs to run a McDonald's or an Applebee's. They could have similar operating costs, or they may have less costs based on volume of products they order. I can only speak on my independent restaurant. Scott and I aren't millionaires. If we were, it wouldn't be based solely on our income from Shakespeare's. It's unfortunate that assumptions are made, acting like all restaurant owners act as slumlords. I am sure they exist, but I am also sure, most of us are as blue-collar as they come.

After the unnamed door guy left the pub, he played against me in a soccer game and slapped me when the ref wasn't looking. He had a head injury from a car accident so it would have been catastrophic if I had retaliated, and really, we are adults, physical altercations shouldn't be a thing. I did verbally confront him after the game and he backed down, like the coward he is. This is as serious as I will ever get in my writing, but it's proof that my life isn't always butterflies and daisies, and I have moments of growth.

Angela and I often run into people who have interacted with this unnamed door guy and his wife. We hear slanderous stories of who we are as people and our business. We have seen social media posts from them saying the quality of our food and drinks have gone down and are different. It is frustrating to be attacked and not react to it, and even more so to let it go.

There are always two sides to a story, and the truth usually falls somewhere in the middle. I debated on even sharing my perception on this person, and whether it was worth the time to let such negativity escape to paper.

I take the time to see the world through other eyes, and wanting to correct any negativity, I hope to focus on the good, and improve myself to support people correctly. I will be the first to tell you, I am not perfect. I learn something new every day on how to be a better person and accept that people who truly aren't good people exist, and there is little I can do about it. That's hard to do without being angry, and I am still working on it, but letting it out is helping. So, thanks to the unnamed former door guy.

You piece of shit.

## So, the Pandemic is over?

The State of Michigan allowed Restaurants to open for a restricted dine-in service officially on June 8$^{th}$, 2020. This news came on Thursday, June 4$^{th}$. Most restaurants in Kalamazoo were not prepared to reopen in 4 days (but good for the Green Top Tavern, who absolutely did!). There came the time for contacting the staff that worked for us 3 months earlier, to see if they still wanted to work for us. Then came following and learning and training the returning employees what guidelines we were to follow. This is what we knew:

When customers entered the pub, they had to have a face mask on until they were seated at a table, then they could take it off.

We had to create hand sanitizer stations available throughout the pub for the public.

Tables were placed 6ft apart from each other and could not be moved for larger parties. 6 people per party was the maximum.

The entire staff had to wear a face cover their entire shift, no matter what position they had.

We were not allowing entry to individuals who showed any signs of illness.

We had a limited returning staff of 25% of the original staff. We did not force anyone to come back out of their comfort zone, and the Government unemployment was paying similar to the returning wages at this time, due to the incentive provided to stay home.

We had to run a limited menu of nachos, pizza, and chicken wings due to staffing shortages. This was not a Shakespeare's problem; this was an industry-wide problem that we still see presently.

This all sounds like it could be a nightmare to run, and if you have read any sort of social media about what it is like to work in a restaurant, then that theory is highly supported. With that said, our customer base was few and far between with people having problems following protocol we had no control over. We did get the occasional, "This is stupid", or "Masks are dumb, and it doesn't make sense" patrons, but they seemed to be people we had never seen making the rounds everywhere just to do so.

The limited menu wasn't a terrible idea. Shakespeare's is known for its Nachos. When we opened our doors in 2003, we had a Con Queso dip that we sold separately from the nachos. It was a deli queso dip we got from a supplier, and it didn't work very well as just a dip, due to oil separation. The taste was fantastic, but the presentation wasn't. We had nachos, but they didn't have queso on them when we first opened, and they just seemed so dry. Then one day, while making myself something to eat, I decided to put the queso on the nachos. This was the missing ingredient to what many people say are their favorite nachos in the world. This was how we were going to make them from now on. It worked so well, that we started seeing posts about them, and soon after, they had more of a following than our craft beer lineup.

A few years later, the deli supplier who made the queso closed its doors permanently, without warning. I had a few cases of queso left, that might last through the week, but a replacement for the queso we used wasn't an option. I had to know what it was. I tracked down the owner of the company and begged him to share or sell me the recipe, which he respectfully declined. I don't give up easily though, so I looked at the ingredients label on the queso we had left, and began doing a "Hell's Kitchen" type, "Taste it, Now Make it" challenge. 3 days later, we had an identical recipe that we now owned. To this day, it is our best culinary masterpiece.

We had door staff at the door whenever we were open now, because of the protocol (Not the unnamed door guy though, he was still afraid to work, but would come in for dinner on a Saturday night). We had outdoor seating, which was a huge hit, because our patio at capacity seated over 125 people, but we limited it to 60 people due to the 6ft social distancing table rule (outdoor seating wasn't considered a capacity limitation). The month of June was just a preparation to see if I could pull off an anniversary party on July 19$^{th}$ of 44 drafts never tapped in Kalamazoo before. If ever there would be a year where it couldn't be done, this would be the year. The Crowler machine of creating canned carry-out drafts was going to be key this year.

Even though we could open for business, many people were still leery about dining out, and people also had gotten accustomed to being home. Breaking that routine was not going to be easy on top of dealing with the fearful possibility of illness. It did seem that restaurants were one of many places considered a breeding house for illness, and there was nothing we could do about that perception except continue to be diligent with strict cleaning measures. Then there were the "Policing" customers, who came to any restaurant and told them they were being "unsafe" when witnessing a dirty table, or a customer who decided to go to the rest room and forget to put their mask on, or added a 7th chair to a table, and the list goes on and on.

Eventually, we knew there would be a COVID exposure that would be reported and covered by the media from a restaurant. We had protocol in place to make decisions for the good of all depending on the situation, but it was a "wait and see" scenario, and if all restaurants could avoid it, we most certainly would. The knowledge of what we were dealing with made that seem impossible, and all we could do is hope we wouldn't be the first to have a reported case so that we can learn how someone else handled it and either mimic it or improve our response from their approach.

On June 23rd, Michigan health officials reported that at least a dozen people who visited a Lansing, Michigan Brew Pub between June 12-20 had tested positive for COVID-19. In just over two weeks from that report, the number had ballooned to more than 180 confirmed cases with 143 of them coming from that same time frame and Brew Pub. A local Kalamazoo bar had employees who had visited Lansing, at that Brew Pub, during that time, and tested positive for COVID-19. Those employees had returned to work with knowledge that they had been exposed, reported it after having worked to the management of the bar, and now this bar had to be the first in Kalamazoo to handle a possible case. I don't know how they went about contacting the Health Department or whether they decided not to until the results of the exposed employees' COVID tests came back. I do know that a Reddit feed was created with the commentary that the current staff of that bar refused to work until those results came back, even though management of the bar was going to continue operating with the possibility of having exposed workers. It was a social media nightmare for that bar, and steps they had taken from a public standpoint were not in the best interest of their employees or their patrons. The week after the news of this Reddit feed came out, Shakespeare's had an exposure case of its own.

I was working, when a bartender came down to my office to tell me one of our co-workers came into work, telling stories of how their roommate was ill and waiting for test results. Immediately, I went upstairs to speak to this employee, and I sent them home, asking that they not return to work until the results of their roommate's test came back. I had the staff deep clean all areas that this employee was exposed to, even though they were in the pub less than 10 minutes. This was not the time to take chances. I called the health department who told me that Shakespeare's had little to worry about if the employee was wearing a mask, which they were, and if I followed protocol, which I was, we were in good standing. I was surprised to hear when inquiring about what to do that even if the employee had tested positive for COVID, I could still allow them to work with the public if they followed all hand washing and mask protocols. It just felt absurd that this was the case, considering the Nation-wide shutdown we had just endured. Shortly after this phone call, I decided it was best to close our doors, and inform the patrons who were in the pub why we were doing so, to be pre-cautionary. I then followed with this post on our Facebook Page,

*"June 27, 2020*

*We will be closing our doors till at least Tuesday, June 30$^{th}$.*

*We received news about one of our employees coming in contact with someone who tested positive for COVID-19.*

*To be clear, NONE OF OUR EMPLOYEES HAVE TESTED POSITIVE FOR COVID-19, AND NO ONE HAS BEEN CONFIRMED TO HAVE BEEN IN THE PUB WHO HAS TESTED POSITIVE FOR COVID-19.*

*We feel it is our responsibility to protect the community that comes into our pub. We will be deep cleaning the pub even more than we have already, and we will contact our County Health Officials about what steps we should take before we open our doors to the public.*

*Our staff member will voluntarily be tested for COVID-19 before returning to work, and if they test positive, we will follow proper guidelines to ensure safety before we open our doors again to the public.*

*We are taking this very seriously and wish to be extra precautionary.*

*Thank you, Kalamazoo for your support and we will post any updates we have as they become available to us.*

*Ted Vadella*

*Co-owner*

*Shakespeare's Pub"*

A few days later, our employee called and told us that his roommate's COVID test came back positive.

I called Scott to let him know the results and discuss what steps we do from here. Scott isn't a social media guy, and rarely pays attention to what social media entails. He asked,

"What do we do? Do we stay closed and wait for our employee's test results? Do we inform the staff?"

Prior to this shift, our employee had not been in the pub for over 5 days, and when they were, they were in for 20 minutes. The staff he was exposed to was not scheduled till at least the next weekend, which was a week away. We didn't need to stay closed and wait.

"We open and hope for the best."

I told Scott.

Days later, it was confirmed that our employee tested positive for COVID-19. Scott revisited his question,

"Ok, what do we do now?"

Having seen what holding health information from the people does, I knew exactly what to do,

"We tell the staff first, then we make an immediate post to the public, sharing it on all possible restaurant support groups that we can to make sure the word is out."

Scott agreed. This wasn't about doing business, or customer service. It was about being a good person, and someone our families would be proud of. With that, I posted this message on Facebook,

*"July 1, 2020,*

*Hello Kalamazoo,*

*We feel the best approach to ensuring the safety of our community is being transparent in how we are handling safety measures towards the fight against COVID-19. Any news that involves our pub, we share with our staff, and then we prepare to share it with our public, immediately.*

*Moments ago, we received a message from a staff member of ours, that they tested positive for COVID-19. This staff member has not been to work for 5 days. When they did come to work, they were at the pub for 20 minutes. We were made aware that they had been in contact with a possible COVID-19 positive individual and we immediately sent them home. At the time of this news, they had not been tested themselves. Before that, they were not in the pub for over 5 days. I share this timeline with you so that you are aware of the amount of exposure this individual had on our public and staff.*

*We spoke to the health department. They assured us that the best approach was following recommendations for the*

*constant use of masks and clean hands throughout our workplace. We also continue to not allow individuals who show signs of illness to work. The majority of our staff that have been in contact with this employee have voluntarily been tested or have set up an appointment to be tested.*

*Again, we will not allow individuals who show signs of illness to work.*

*It is important that our community knows what is going on, and we feel morally obligated to share it with you. You should have all the information we can give before you make a decision to spend time at our pub.*

*Thank you, Kalamazoo, for everything.*

*As always, we hope you stay safe.*

*Ted Vadella*

*Co-owner*

*Shakespeare's Pub"*

We were now in a waiting period of how the public would assess our sharing of information. The local news covered it, a restaurant support group with a massive following allowed us to post the message, and to their credit, they policed the comments of negativity, even asking me if I was ok with them. I told them to let people ask questions and make comments, I was an adult and would handle them as they came. I was expecting far worse to come of this, because the question of opening with COVID numbers not dwindling at the rate health officials were hoping was taken into consideration but being a small business owner with an uncertainty to whether we could continue to put ourselves at financial ruin also was at the forefront of our minds. Scott and I both had families to feed. Within minutes, we were seeing the reaction of our community, and it was overwhelmingly supportive.

We were thanked for our transparency. We were shown support by others saying this is how you set the precedence of reinforcing safe practices. We also were attacked for staying open, even after our transparency and recommendations from the county health officials. Like most social media commentary, there is going to be venomous debate amongst its audience, and for that, most people defended us, but even so, we were transparent with those that didn't like our decision to stay open. As I have gotten older, I realize more and more that I am going to have to confront and approach uncomfortable situations where I must make a decision that could possibly be unpopular, or quite possibly wrong. I take my time, if possible, not to make a quick decision, and I try very hard to do what's right every time. I am not prideful enough to stick to convictions if I have heard the fault in their logic. This is something I have learned as I have aged. What once was a cocky, arrogant late 20's bar owner is now a reasonable, faulty family man who can sleep well at night knowing that I meant for the best, and even in failing to do so, I can learn to do it right in the future. I feel confident this was the right decision, and we were supported with dine-in customers and carry-out orders increasing from our transparency.

I don't know that I can take credit for the approach of other local businesses who also in latter days had to admit to COVID positive exposures, but the wording they used are very similar to what I posted on July 1$^{st}$,2020. Either way, Kalamazoo was supportive to not only Shakespeare's, but to all restaurants that shared with such transparency. It amazes me that this model of honesty that restaurants shared isn't used more often in our government politics, but that is another story.

I was now a little over 2 weeks away from our 17$^{th}$ Anniversary, and the realism of not wanting to create a mass gathering, but still give our community hope that we would be able to see one eventually seemed important. Nothing was the same, as far annual traditions. Oberon Day was cancelled by Bell's earlier in the year, as was all of the city St. Patrick's Day celebrations.

I started contacting breweries back in January to see if they could do a draft for us for July 19th, expecting to hear that they wouldn't be able to this year, but I was pleasantly surprised to hear the opposite. The craft beer world was looking forward to gathering again, and that meant testing out small events. The seasonal beer festivals were still cancelled for the remainder of the year, and although off-premise (an industry term for alcohol purchases that are made at grocery stores and specialty shops to be consumed at home) was having record sales, on-premise would need a lot of help. On July 11$^{th}$, 2020, I was able to post the 44 drafts never before tapped in Kalamazoo;

THE LIST:

1. Espresso Cream Soda-Northwoods Sodas
2. Ay Caramba- Witch's Hat Brewing
3. Margarita Gose-Cigar City Brewing
4. Gerald's 2nd Birthday Cake- Tantrick Brewing
5. Health Care Heroes- Big Lake Brewing
6. Take it Wit Cha- One Well Brewing
7. Citra Obsession- Rockford Brewing
8. DayMaus- Old Nation Brewing
9. Ransack the Universe- Collective Arts Brewing
10. La Petite Deth- Revolution Brewing
11. Peanuts & Crackerjack- Mitten Brewing
12. Buzzy Joose- Blackrocks Brewing
13. Hop Grandslam 2020- Bell's Brewing
14. Tequila Barrel Flamingo Fruit Fight-Bell's Brewing
15. BBA Chocolate Cherry Vanilla Stout- Bell's Brewing
16. My Nirvana- New Belgium Brewing
17. Fleeting Violet- New Belgium Brewing
18. UK Springbreak- New Belgium Brewing
19. Err on the Side of Awesome- New Belgium Brewing
20. La Folie Grand Reserve Honey & Saffron- New Belgium Brewing
21. Shortsicle- Short's Brewing
22. All Together IPA- Short's Brewing
23. Aqua Bear- Short's Brewing
24. Tenacious E- Short's Brewing
25. The Short Table- Short's Brewing
26. Fruit Punch Seltzer- Odd Side Ales
27. Pink Lemonade Seltzer- Odd Side Ales
28. I Love it when you call me Big Papaya- Odd Side Ales
29. Deleterious Nitro- Odd Side Ales

30. Zangief's Bearhug Nitro- Short's Brewing
31. Spiney Norman, Spiney- Right Brain Brewing
32. Sherbert Hoover Raspberry Vanilla- Presidential Brewing
33. Fresh Squeezed Old Fashioned- Deschutes Brewing
34. Planete Plum- Deschutes Brewing
35. Soul Mate- Tapistry Brewing
36. Gravity Flux- Ellison Brewing
37. Pineapple Chili Kombucha- Flying Embers
38. ACE Mango Cider- ACE Ciders
39. Windfall Cider- ACE Ciders
40. Moblin- Starcut Ciders
41. Apple Pie Cider- Sierra Rose Ciders
42. Wynona's Big Brown Ale- Voodoo Brewing
43. Love Child- Voodoo Brewing
44. Trail Lyte Raspberry- Arbor Brewing

We stuck to the protocol given to us by the State of Michigan and had a line with 6ft. markers as not to crowd people who waited to come in. We sold a lot of Crowlers that day, paying off the purchase of the machine. I felt productive and accomplished again. The staff working told me they felt a little of the magic of what we were before the pandemic, and it was a welcomed change from the slow crowds we had been seeing. I didn't realize how much I had missed doing my job within the community as I did this day. It didn't go down as a record-breaking sales day for the anniversary, but it does rank up there with one of our most memorable. I have said it many times before, and I will say it again here, thank you to the craft breweries and Kalamazoo people for all the years you have supported Shakespeare's.

## Going through the motions

After July 19th, we thought the next thing to look forward to would be the kids returning for school, but that appeared to be something we would not see much of either. Virtual attendance was still held in high regard. Professional and collegiate sports had taken a hit, with the cancellation of the March Madness NCAA tournament for basketball, and a shortened NBA season that resulted in a surreal summer playoff held in a bubble at Disney World. Professional sports looked weird on tv without the fans, which made for an altered experience that you didn't know was so important. Football, however, the way it is filmed, was still very entertaining and helped us feel a little return to normal for all the sporting fans over the years at the pub.

I tapped an Oktoberfest for the first time ever, before September because how the year had panned out so far, nothing was normal. We usually held a Harvest Day with 44 drafts of nothing but Hard Cider, Pumpkin Ales, Oktoberfests, and Meads, but with restricted occupancy numbers, we cancelled it due to its niche time frame that we weren't sure we could sell all the product before it wasn't Fall weather anymore (No one wants an Oktoberfest in November). We did start to see an increase in business, even hitting the 50% mark on weekends easily. All this was happening, and staff started to return, but the COVID-19 numbers were increasing at an alarming rate again, and the talk of a second restaurant lockdown was inevitable before the annual Black Friday shopping event for retailers. A part of me was worried about it, because we are self-employed, but there was also a part of me that wanted the break for Christmas. My brother is a Software

Engineer and had been for the better part of 30 years. He is in a position now that he takes the entire month of December off, and sometimes starting as early as mid-November. I didn't mind the idea of sitting in and hibernating with my family during the cold months.

On November 18, 2020, restaurants in Michigan were asked to stop dine in service and return to carry out only. We are a very large pub and carry-out is not something that would support what we do, so we decided we would wait out the lockdown again. It was time to go home for an uncertain time, but this time, I knew a system to get me through...

## Hallmark Christmas Movies

*"Day 1… the sequel!*

*My wife prepared for this shut down by informing the neighbors that we don't need Oreos purchased for us… this seems very mean… and tactical… but it's ok… because…*

*I bought 4 dozen cookies online, then I called "The Hipster Chipster Cookie Company" and ordered 2 dozen more… and also… my mother is staying with us, and she makes cookie trays for the holidays… she makes 12 different cookies…*

*But I guess there aren't any Oreos…*

*I call this foreplay…. My wife would call it something else…*

*I bought a home gym that required assembly… it took 2.5 Hallmark Christmas movies to assemble… I did this last Thursday… it looks like a nice set… someday I may use it for its intended purpose… but it has a cushy seat and a good view of the tv…*

*My 8-year-old is back to virtual learning starting today… and my wife worked last night… so already, I started the day off with the possibility of being in trouble…*

*I still don't understand the difference between a verb and an adjective…"*

*"Day 2…*

*My wife whispered in my ear before bed, "Do you want to exercise tomorrow?"*

*I said yes… but she didn't specify what time… so I may have missed my window, to avoid it properly…*

*I bought wall climbers on Amazon for the kittens… I am not sure where the studs on the wall are, so if they aren't strong enough to hold, it's going to cause trust issues…*

*Rowan is supposed to be in school learning about jellyfish… but there is a new Star Wars Christmas show on Disney+… so his "teacher" is making today an A/V Day…*

*I may have ordered too many cookies for Thanksgiving… so I will probably have to eat some today to make room for the ones coming next week… responsibility is hard as an adult…*

*I put on jeans today… I am out of practice of quarantine habits… my sweatpants aren't even dirty…*

*I think I am going to put up the Christmas tree…"*

*"Day 3…*

*I picked up cookies last night that are supposed to last until Thanksgiving… there is a part of me that thinks I should call and order more… but there is my wife who may think otherwise…*

*Rowan at dinner was contemplating life last night… one of his "Rowan-isms" was "I guess Santa Claus works 3rd shift on Christmas."*

*He's not wrong…*

*I didn't put up the Christmas tree last night… I think it will happen this morning…*

*I did wind up exercising last night… but my wife asked, 'are you done already?", when I came upstairs… so maybe I didn't exercise after all…*

*My mother had never seen the movie, "Bridesmaids", so we watched it last night… I sometimes forget she's in her 80's and might find this humor inappropriate… but I argue back that she has read Harlequin romance novels my entire life and took me to see "Flash Dance" when I was 9… so she doesn't have a compelling argument to make based on this history…"*

*"Day 4…*

*The routine of positivity my wife attempted to display during the first pandemic lockdown are trying to seep into this round of days… She is motivated to exercise on a daily basis, only to be sidetracked by my small and devilish suggestions… Today, I blame my mother, who wanted pizza for lunch… so I must respect my elders…*

*I discovered a website called "Goldbelly" today… they have food from restaurants and bakeries found all over the country. While scrolling their cookie selection, I found a* *bakery who offers 4 cookies for $39... That's $9.75 a cookie... I don't think I can justify their purchase...*

*I had sweatpants on and switched to jeans... still not in pro form for this shutdown...*

*I think I may be able to order the $10 cookies...*

*My mother's dog is usually afraid of my dog, but realized my dog is blind, so she is now bullying my dog... I should be upset, but my dog is the worst... and even blind, if it came down to it, my money's on her...*

*My wife left the room... I'm going to order these cookies..."*

My mother stayed in seclusion for 9 months in her little condo with not much contact from other living people during the first shutdown, and even further in after the restaurant ban was abolished. The elderly were given grave concern to not be in contact with many people. It was comforting to know that my mother valued life enough to be safe, because I can't tell you how many times she hinted that she was ready to go over the years. She had a 3lb. mini yorkie named Izzy that kept her company for the better part of the last decade. This dog meant as much to her as her own children. In fact, when you visited, she had pictures of my children, my family, my sister, and my brother and his family in pockets throughout the condo. The dog had a picture in every room.

When the holidays come around, mom had been spending Thanksgiving and Christmas with us for the past 3 years instead of being home closer to my brother and sister. She would stay for a month or so and leave promptly after New Year's. My mother makes the world's best Pierogi's, a Polish dumpling of cheese and potato boiled in butter and topped with salt and sour cream as a condiment. We had her make them every year around this time, along with the dozens of cookie trays she made for friends and family.

My mother complained about it but wouldn't pass it up for the opportunity to make others happy. Funny how that it, saying you don't want to do something, but enjoy doing it anyway.

I always waited for my mother to put up the Christmas tree and decorate for the holidays, because growing up, this time of year was always the best in our home. Christmas is a feeling like no other, where for brief pockets of time, you are more aware of the life you have and people you share it with, and it's a great thing. My wife loved to decorate the Christmas tree every year, making an event of it with popcorn garland, hot chocolate, and Christmas music. My eldest son grew out of it as he became a teenager, but we forced him to participate any way. That is how the discovery of Hallmark Christmas movies came about in our home.

I was scanning the television in hopes of finding something festive to watch while decorating in place of the old time Christmas classics, and that Mariah Carey song. I came across a movie about a shoe addict who loved Christmas staring one of the girls from "Full House" and it was so cheesy and bad. My family groaned that I put it on, but as they were busy trying to get through the decorating, I would catch them paying attention to the tv, more so than what ornaments they were putting up. They will never admit that they watched as intently as they did, but it was enough for me.

After that first year, Hallmark channel started advertising that they would have 30 new movies for the holidays each year, across two different Hallmark channels and an app for your phone that would make calendar reminders for you. There was a good 5 year stretch of new content worth watching, and my wife pointing out how each plot line was so similar, and that the set pieces were obviously done on one stage for each, but what do you expect from such low budget stuff?

## The Cutting Board

*"Day 5...*

*It never fails when you are on a limited time schedule that your wife says the sentence, "I have to use the bathroom really quick."*

*In my experience, "really quick" can be estimated between 15 minutes and a viewing of "The Lord of the Rings- Extended cut." ...*

*Blane's Farm & Fleet is a hidden gem for holiday junk food... No other place feels completely normal to buy a crossbow and peanut brittle quite like Blane's...*

*I didn't get a crossbow... I did get peanut brittle...*

*This morning, I checked Best Buy for a new Xbox... it was in stock, so I bought it... my card was denied... because my bank thought the purchase was sketchy... I approved the charge... Best Buy said, "Please wait" instead of allowing me to purchase... and then returned with the prompt, "This item is no longer available" ... sometimes it's better to live dangerously... at least that's what I am going to tell my bank on Monday...*

*Chocolate oranges have no business tasting as good as they do...*

*I got my Christmas tree up... Rowan and I put up the ornaments... I noticed this morning that the ornaments had been rearranged for better clarity... I can't decide if it was my mother or my wife who did this... probably a combination of both...*

*It turns out, Best Buy has charged me for an Xbox and says they will have it in stock soon for me to pick up... I sure hope this is true..."*

*"Day 6...*

*I got out all of my outside Christmas lights from storage... but then my wife needed Excedrin Migraine and my mother wanted McDonald's... It's only 1pm, but if I procrastinate 2 more hours, I'll run out of daylight...*

*I thought I figured out a sneaky way to order Kelvin and Co. by just ordering individual meats instead of combos... but then when it was delivered in 4 boxes and 2 bags, I still felt judged... I ate it, but I left a little pulled pork... I feel less judged...*

*I didn't order the 4 cookies for $40... but then I am being persuaded to order from a friend of ours... I think I can sell this to my wife that we need more...*

*I don't know where the extension cords are... so I can't put up the outside lights anyway...*

*Happy Monday..."*

*"Day 7...*

*Rowan has art class and we, as parents, have to give guidance on creating an alligator balloon animal... my wife goes into this with positivity and a willingness to make it fun... at best, I can make stick figures... I think I'm going to sit this one out...*

*I overestimated the amount of cookies a family of 5 can consume on Thanksgiving... estimating 3 dozen for each person, I don't know whether to accept defeat or treat it as a challenge... this is what I approach with positivity and a willingness to make it fun compared to the healthiness my wife endorses... we both have our strengths as a couple...*

*The alligator art project is at the cutting out stage... Rowan has asked for my help...*

*I debate whether today is the best day to go shopping for green bean casserole ingredients... it seems like Thanksgiving is the only day I must contemplate this...*

*Maybe smaller scissors would be best to cut this alligator out...*

*Do I really need a pumpkin pie?*

*I think so..."*

*"Day 8...*

*I bought a cookie dough dip, pumpkin pie, and a 3-berry pie today... my argument in favor of 2 pies is that we have a full container of Cool Whip... and 1 pie isn't enough to use it all...*

*The cookie dough dip was for the cookies to dip in... just in case the cookies needed more cookie...*

*This is home economics at its finest... it's unfortunate that it isn't one of the virtual school classes my son takes... although, some may argue I am doing it wrong...*

*Rowan is excited about the Lions having a better record tomorrow... it's nice to see such positivity towards our football team as such a young age... they haven't broken him yet..."*

*"Day 9...*

*Thanksgiving...*

*I'd like to take the time to thank those of you who have supported my efforts and thanks to those of you who didn't support them, but didn't hinder my progress...*

*I still have a second pie, peanut butter balls, and caramel turtles...To scale this view, this is a whole pumpkin pie...*

*The worst part about this picture? My wife has Covid and the only symptom she has is loss of taste and smell... on Thanksgiving... Guess she won't appreciate all that she has fully...."*

A few years ago, my wife asked me to go shopping with her mother, my mother, and herself at a place called, "Home Goods". I have no idea why she would want me to go out on a girl's shopping trip to a place that has home furnishings, but my guess is so that I can have an opinion as to what goes or fits in our home, and if that opinion does not match that of my wife, I will see that my opinion is of little importance, which really is ok, because my wife has good taste.

Immediately, upon arriving at the store, the 3 of them left me to my own devices. All alone in a store, without supervision. I have many unnecessary material cravings in my life other than sugary food, and one of those things are cutting boards. Home Goods had a section of kitchen gadgets, and low and behold, there was an entire aisle of weird or unique shaped wooden serving boards. Among these boards, was a rounded spatula-like serving board as big as a table. No one in their right mind needs such a board, and the price of $100 didn't justify that it was a necessary purchase either. However, I was alone.

I scoped out which aisles my family was in. They were close. I was going to have to sneak past them as quietly as I could, while they were distracted, as to not see me make my way to the register. It was going to be tough. Obscenely large cutting board under arm, I made my way softly and silently out of the aisle. I peeked around the corner of the next aisle where my wife and mother-in-law were checking out some coffee mugs they could get as small Christmas gifts. My mother was semi-interested, and

I thought maybe enough to where she wouldn't be paying attention to my whereabouts. I was wrong. My mother has a built-in radar that tracks her children's movements. Something I thought may have expired as we became adults, but as time would tell, it was still working up to factory standards. She turned and made eye-contact with me. My eyes widening and my tiptoe pace increasing, I had hoped she would get the hint to not acknowledge me. She giggled. It was enough to stop my wife from what she was doing and look up. I was caught.

My wife, asking the most asked question of our entire relationship, with a semi-disgusted, yet intrigued curiosity,

"What are you doing?"

"I found this board and thought it would be great for entertaining?",

I am not as good at debate as I once was and thought for sure she wasn't going to buy it. Her reactionary question wasn't what I was expecting, but rather, inquisitive,

"Where would we put it? It's too big for a cupboard."

"I can make a hanger on the side of the wall, it will be a decorative conversation piece.",

I surprised myself with the answer.

"How much is it?",

Angela asked the question that I was hoping to avoid answering.

"It's more than I really want to spend.", I left it at that, rather than even revealing its price, and returned it to its place with the other cutting boards.

We shopped down aisles of rugs, and pillows, and small trinkets. I was using my phone, not really paying attention. My wife looked up and broke me out of my daydream with the question,

"Where's your mom?"

I had no idea, but this little grandmother of 5 was wondering aimlessly, would be my guess, in aisles of trinkets that interested her. I was wrong again. A quick glance at the register, and my mother had found a "Nice Young Man" as she often referred to store clerks that helped her, to carry the giant cutting board to the front. She had already paid for it, and there was no turning back. We now owned the largest cutting board known to man. I hung it on a dining room wall, just as I said I would, and we have used it every Thanksgiving, Mother's Day, Christmas, and New Year's since.

The cutting board on Thanksgiving is usually used for charcuterie-type meat and cheese and crackers before the turkey is done. This year, it was to be used to display all the cookies and pies I had purchased leading up to the big day. My wife started making Turkey for the family every year, about 5 years prior. I was reluctant to try, being that traditionally, my mother and Angela's mother always made a nice spread of Thanksgiving necessities, and I didn't want to mess up what was already perfect. My wife really wanted to do this.

The first time she made a turkey, one of my brother-in-law's came up for the big day. I was closing the pub the Wednesday before, and industry-wide, Thanksgiving Eve is considered the busiest bar night of the year. Scott and I would switch year-to-year, so that we could spend time with our families. As busy as that night is for the bars and restaurants, it's generally a nightmare to deal with from a management view. Hundreds of people gather, in a place they either haven't been to in a very long time or have never been to and their families frequent. For whatever reason, when people gather at places they aren't familiar with, they tend to treat the establishment like it's substitute teacher day in high school.

They stand rather than sit at tables, causing a problem for the staff to get through, and they will argue with that. At any given time, someone from the party may overindulge, are then cut off from drinking further, and someone in the party they are with tries to sneak them alcohol. If they get caught, they are asked to leave. They either understand, say sorry and do so, or they argue and leave, but make sure they get the last word, or they threaten to call the owner and not pay for how they are being treated. I have seen all 3, but rarely do I see the first option. Thankfully, it isn't everyone, but the select few that do this are the most memorable. After a night like this, as we close our doors and clean up, all I ever do is look forward to getting home and sleeping in till it's time to entertain people. This year, I get a text at 2:45am with a picture of my brother-in-law, three sheets to the wind drunk, posing with his head over a turkey body. This first turkey is going to be horrible, I thought. I was wrong, again.

I got home, and magically, my house was quiet. Not even 30 minutes had gone by since that text and they had retreated to bed. 4 hours later, my wife's alarm went off, she was up, and preparing and basting the turkey further in the oven. She was dedicated. We ate that first turkey cooked by my wife at noon that day, and it was everything a turkey should be. She has been cooking them ever since.

The Thanksgiving of COVID though, she was preparing the turkey the night before as she normally did, cutting onions, and using a lemon juice when she realized, she couldn't smell it. She called me into the room,

"Ted, can you come here?"

Entering the kitchen thinking I was going to have to open a jar or do something "husbandy",

"What's up?"

"Taste this.",

she asked, giving me the broth she was making to baste the turkey with.

"It's good.",

I thought she was looking for.

"You taste it?",

looking puzzled she asked.

"Yeah, it's good.",

I thought she needed to hear it again.

"I can't taste it. Or smell it.",

Angela announced to me in a surprised realization.

I knew immediately, this was going to ruin Thanksgiving.

After 10 minutes of checking if she was feeling congested, or feverish, or any of the other tell-tale signs of COVID, we concluded that it was just a mild case, but had to call family who were planning on coming to cancel their trip. I immediately started power eating cookies, taking in half a dozen fist-sized chocolate chips in a couple of minutes.

"What are you doing?",

my wife asked.

"If it's COVID, I am going to enjoy these until I can't.",

I pronounced with certain defeat coming.

She woke up the next morning, still prepping turkey and sides for the immediate family that was under our roof. My mother was with us, and what are the chances she visits, and we get COVID while she has avoided it the whole time? She was skeptical about it because my wife was fine other than symptoms we couldn't detect as outsiders and refused to eat dinner without my wife. My wife didn't sit, always making excuses not to be at the table, and my mother didn't notice. At about 5:30 Thanksgiving night, while serving myself a heaping pile of mashed potatoes, gravy, and corn, I realized that it was just mushy in my mouth, and there was no flavor. I had lost my sense of taste.

The next day, my mother went to the couch, and slept. All day. She wasn't feverish, but she was tired. So tired. I was planning on taking her out of the house if we made it through Thanksgiving to not expose her if it was serious, but it was too late. She was in it. By the end of the day, she had a small fever, but her breathing was fine. I woke her to ask her if she was ready for bed, and she looked me dead in the eye,

"Ok, I am. I don't see me getting through this. I don't know that I will be here tomorrow. Good night, honey.",

and like that, my mother went to bed.

This is how my mother says things without thought. I spent the night listening to hear her breath, thankfully she snores, but each time the snoring stopped, I was wide-eyed checking. The next morning, she woke up with energy and the sniffles. She was coming out of it already. We went and got the drive thru COVID tests. The results came 4 days later. My mother surely had COVID, but she was already over the scary phase. My taste and smell returned after 4 days. My wife lost her sense of taste and smell for 6 weeks. COVID is a strange disease. My 80-year-old, just out of breast cancer treatment, mother had 24 hours of symptoms, and people much younger than her with much better health were dying. Maybe we will never know why it affects people differently. One of life's many mysteries.

## My Edible Experience

*"Day 10...*

*It's quite possible that I may have eaten too many cookies... so I switched to Doritos...*

*I watched the Beastie Boys Documentary on Apple TV+ last night... my wife and I were subconsciously dancing to ourselves... this is life in your 40's... playing "Fishdom" while bobbing in your head to old school rap music that still has it...*

*I have never played "Fishdom", but my wife has put in the time for both of us...*

*My youngest son and I have been playing catch with the football... he keeps trying to convince me the reason he misses sometimes is because I haven't bought him football gloves... then he winks and says in a whisper, "Christmas" ... I think I need to teach him subtlety, or maybe, I have?*

*The whisper kind of makes it subtle, doesn't it?"*

*"Day 11...*

*Playing pass with the football seems to be Rowan's new favorite pastime with Dad... he even practices touchdown dance celebrations... this is the time I always hope his mother isn't looking out the window...*

*However, she should know I didn't teach him hip gyrations... but someone had to... or maybe it is hereditary... my wife is a pretty good dancer...*

*The pickle ornament always makes me laugh on the tree... "Hide the Pickle" is an actual thing for Christmas time... Be careful when you google, "Hide the Pickle."*

*"Day 12...*

*I started regrowing my beard... I am usually the most predictable person, but sometimes I'm mysterious... or lazy...*

*I finished putting up Christmas lights outside... my neighbor's house is much better... I think I may make an arrow of lights pointing at their house... I accept defeat and give credit where it is due...*

*I find that I can eat a snickerdoodle cookie and wonder why I don't eat them more often, but then 2 cookies in, I never want to eat them again... chocolate chip doesn't make me feel the same...*

*I saw a toothbrush today that also is a water pic at the same time... Water pics are messy... Adding toothpaste to the mix?*

*I kind of want one..."*

*"Day 13...*

*Rowan is doing Bible study and he exclaims that "the Bible is lying" ...*

*I believe in God, although I am not as educated about religion as I should be, but I am pretty sure that it is frowned upon to say the Bible is lying, for those in the know...*

*My dog has really responded to CBD oil for her glaucoma... it makes me want to try an edible again... but with the real stuff... because I weigh more...*

*I started burning wood in my outdoor fire bowl yesterday... I asked that a football not be thrown by it... Rowan listened... my wife did not...*

*Positive note... Nerf footballs are not that flammable...*

*I debate on turning Animal Crossing on... I haven't checked my island since the end of the last lockdown... I imagine I have a cockroach infestation..."*

*"Day 14...*

*Door Dash said I could get free delivery from Little Caesars... who am I to say no to a deal like that?*

*I stopped going to Water Street Coffee years ago because a Barista was calling me "White Chocolate Mocha" and I realized I had a problem... but a friend of mine reminded me how good their coffee is and it's all I want now...*

*80's movies are not kid friendly, even if they were for kids in the 80's... as 80's kids, we were lucky or abused depending on how you look at it… I don't advise watching "The Wizard" with Fred Savage with a 2nd Grader…*

*I bought enough pizza to have dinner too…*

*It's December 1st and I think I may have overdosed on Hallmark Christmas movies already…*

*This shutdown is killing me…"*

Riley, the chihuahua, was starting to show signs of glaucoma, which was a side effect from her diabetes. We knew it was coming, but her little eyes were starting to bulge and look deep red. It looked very painful. She still showed signs that her sight wasn't completely gone, and the vet suggested we consider surgery to remove her eyes so that she would be more comfortable. Riley was 12 at this time, and with all the health problems she was running into, we didn't think it was the best option to put her under only to wake up without any vision. She was already such a fighter, and the anxiety she naturally had as a chihuahua broke my heart to think she would be so confused. My wife did what my wife does, and researched alternatives to help her. My wife doesn't scan articles, she turns it into a PhD program of study to make sure the options presented are feasible and possible. CBD and THC treatments for pets with glaucoma were humane and effective. It certainly didn't show signs of further hurting Riley, so all we would lose was time between this and a surgery if it didn't work.

The number of medicinal shops in Kalamazoo and the surrounding area is infinite. Only outnumbered by gas stations and certainly giving credit unions a run for their money in terms of availability. We were only able to find 2 with options for pets and going in and having a "Budtender" help choose the correct dosage was comical. Here are all these people getting stuff for themselves, and here I am getting stuff for a blind chihuahua. 50mg was the recommended dose, but they had 300mg. Pet shops, who just started carrying CBD for pets with joint issues had a 15mg dosage. The Budtender said it wouldn't hurt the chihuahua to have such a large dose but might make her sleepy.

The directions suggested 2 servings a day. This worked well, because we added it to her dry food. Small doses at first, which didn't seem to be making much impact. We went on full force, with 300mg, and within days, her eyes started to bulge less, and the deep redness they had faded to a cloudy blindness as expected. She was now fully blind, but spunky, and angry just as she always had been. She knew her surroundings and day to day life wasn't as terrible as we thought it would be. We had to block the basement staircase with a baby gate so she wouldn't fall down them. It happened a couple of times, and to Riley's credit, she would lay flat on her stomach, and slide down, making her pick up speed but have less impact when she reached the bottom. She once caught a scent of random popcorn kernels on the basement floor and decided to slide to where she thought they might be, time and time again, even after my wife had brought her up. This is when it became necessary to have the baby gate, because once she was downstairs, she could no longer make her way back up the stairs by herself. She seemed to have so much more control over who she was now that the pain seemed to have subsided from the glaucoma. CBD was a miracle in this instance, and I was happy we went with it instead of surgery. On another note, the suggested serving of 15mg versus the 300mg that Riley was taking, and that she still didn't sleep all day shows my dog would have been an unbelievably high tolerance pot head as a human.

As previously stated, I had many knee surgeries, and a clinical trial that ended with me losing all the cartilage in my hips because of a massive amount of calcium buildup. A side effect that I helped discover for this clinical trial (Yay!). I also decided to forgo surgery, so that I could continue to play soccer, which I loved. The set back to that was, I am not the kind of person who takes medication if I can avoid it, and after each soccer game the pain was so intense, I would groan most of the night. My wife put up with it but wasn't happy to see me in pain. Over the years, many of our friends that we interacted with at the pub had given us many samples of THC edibles to help me with it. I have never taken a drug, nor have I even smoked a single cigarette, a badge of honor I wear proudly, so the idea of taking an edible, even though it was legal, and it was to help me with my pain seemed like a bad idea. Then, on one random soccer Thursday, my wife got sick of my groaning and insisted I try an edible. Against my better judgement I agreed, and if anything, it made for a decent story.

We were watching "Friends", a show that we watch when we are too lazy to find something new to watch and just want the television on. My wife went to our bathroom and grabbed a very long, fruit-roll up like gummy bear. She tore a piece off and handed it to me. I was watching the TV so when she handed it to me, I ate it. She was reading some directions, and looked to me and said,

"Ok, where is it?"

"Where's what?"

I asked, never taking my eyes off the TV.

"Where's IT!",

Angela emphasized.

"Oh, I ate it.",

I thought she would be proud.

"You ate all of it?!",

in a panicking manner, my wife looked at me.

"Yeah, you handed it to me."

"You were supposed to eat a quarter of that!"

I could see at this moment, that my wife was jogging what to do through her head. I wasn't sure if I was supposed to panic as well or wait and see what she thought. This was the Thanksgiving episode of "Friends" the one with the "Gellar Cup", and I was more focused on that then what I ate.

"Ok.", she said. "I am going to take the same portion size, because I have been through this, and then maybe I can help you to get through it better."

The logic seemed substantial. Angela smoked pot at the beginning of our relationship, so I assume she probably did a lot more before we were together. Plus, I trusted her. She made the majority of our adult decisions. She tore a piece off, ate it, and went to take a shower.

About 20 minutes later, my bathroom door opens, and my wife pops her head out of the door, making eye contact with me, and says,

"Are you ok?"

I was starting to get comfortable, focused mainly on the apparent "Friends" marathon that was going on and hadn't thought about my hip or what I ingested since Angela left the room. It hit me then,

"You know, I don't really feel different, but my hip isn't bothering me."

My wife, wide eyed, small smile, focuses on me and reveals about herself,

"I'm stoned."

Funny, I thought. Here I am, never having done a drug in my life and not really feeling "stoned" but relaxed, and my experienced wife comes out and says she is higher than a kite.

I have heard that many people react differently to being high. Some get relaxed and say very little. Some get philosophical and say things that aren't as deep as they think they are. Then some get energetic and start performing tasks they always wanted to get to. My wife is the latter. Soon after she asked me if I was ok, I turned the light off and went to sleep. Angela stayed up till 4am cleaning and vacuuming. I heard none of this. That is, until 4am, shortly after Angela went to bed, when Bob the Cat wanted to go outside, and the blind chihuahua had to go potty.

I remember waking and walking down the hallway to the living room slider. It was very tunnel vision-like with a little spinning. Spinning like being drunk but not to the extent where I may vomit. Just subtle. Light. I remember opening the slider door, but the next thing I knew, I was now standing in front of a toilet. I assume I went pee, because I was in the right position to do so, but I didn't have to go anymore. Did I go? I don't know. There was a slight panic over this. What was going on? It was 4am. I took the edible about 10:30pm. Surely it couldn't still be working. Could it? I went back to sleep, knowing I had to be up in 2 hours to get my 8-year-old ready for school.

My alarm went off at 6am. My wife, who had just gone to bed about 3 hours earlier, was fast asleep, and would have been no use helping get our 2$^{nd}$ grader ready for school. Rowan always woke with the sound of my alarm as well, and he is a morning person if there ever was one. The minute he gets out of bed, all smiles and questions. I am usually receptive to this, but not THIS morning.

"Dad, I'm really good at basketball. I hit 3-pointers and layoffs all the time.", he said.

"They are called layups",

still trying to be a good father and teach him something.

"No, they are layoffs",

he confidently stated.

"They are layups.",

I dead eye looked him in his face so that he knew I wasn't joking.

“Maybe when you were young they were.”, Rowan mumbled.

I didn’t have it in me to continue this banter, so I raised my hand ever so slightly in front of me as if I was trying to surrender,

“Rowan can we just be quiet this morning? Dad isn’t feeling the best.”, I pleaded.

I will always give my son credit, he isn’t one to push me when he knows I need the time, and he just sat, waiting for his breakfast, which on days like today, he knew was going to be microwaved pancakes. 2 minutes later, there would be 2 light and fluffy stacks of 3 pancakes each topped with warm syrup and whipped cream. Rowan’s absolute favorite meal.

While he was eating his breakfast, I went to get ready for work. I felt so groggy, and unfocused, but high strung from not being completely in control of my surroundings. “What the hell did people want to feel like this for?”, I thought. I brushed my teeth, but it took longer to concentrate on each tooth, and brushed my hair, put on deodorant. Got dressed. It was all very doable but in slow motion. I had to get Rowan to the bus stop, but I was certain it couldn’t be like this.

The bus stop was across the street at my neighbor’s house. It was wintertime, so I had the excuse to tell Rowan I wouldn’t be able to sit out there with him today, but I would watch him from the window. It was cold. He understood, and was happy about it, because it always made him feel a little more adult when he could do things without his parents right next to him. I just couldn't imagine if another adult tried to make small talk with me if I could keep up. This was the best for everyone if I didn't try. The bus came, and Rowan waved to me as he got on. I made it! It was beer line cleaning day though. Which meant I had to get to work to meet the line cleaners. My house isn't terribly far from downtown Kalamazoo, or the pub, but it is still far enough to where I was questioning if I could drive. Or if I should. Was I drunk? No. My motor skills were intact. Did I have good reaction time? I decided I could take a backroad there, straight shot, not heavy traffic, and I would be in the clear. The drive was easy, because of the tunnel vision and heightened awareness of my surroundings, I was probably more cautious than ever. Pulling into the pub parking lot again, the sense of accomplishment came over me. I made it!

I got out of the car, and Bob, my trusty beer line cleaning guy met me in the parking lot,

"Hey Ted, how's it going?"

I turned to Bob, and hand motioned towards him, but no words were coming out. I didn't know that though. I thought I was saying a lot of things. I realized I wasn't when Bob just stood there and looked at me confused. Words started to formulate, it just took a little more concentration,

"I had an edible last night"

Bob immediately understood and the confused look turned to compassion,

"Oh, what time?"

"10:30?",

I responded, thinking he would think I am such a light weight.

"How much did you take?!",

Bob asked.

"Apparently more than I should have?", I confusingly answered.

Bob was the man with the plan,

"Ok, we are going to go inside. You go sleep it off in the office, and we will do the lines, I'll come get you when we are done."

"OK!",

I excitedly responded.

This was a great idea! I was just going to go in the office. Wait it out. Down the stairs to the kitchen, we turned the alarm off, and Bob went to work. I opened my office door, which was right off the kitchen line, and positioned the chairs so that I could get comfortable, the problem became, I forgot why I was in there, and when I remembered, I had too much anxiety to sleep. Was I going to be able to work through a lunch shift? Would this wear off in time? What do I do if it doesn't?

I focused and looked at the schedule for the morning. My veteran cook of 5 years, Joel, was coming in at 9am. He would be there with me till 10:30am when we opened, and before any other staff would be in. Joel was in a band, surely, he would know what to do. I waited. The clock seemed to stop moving. Finally, I heard the kitchen door open, and excitedly I opened the office door to find out, Joel had given his shift to the 19-year-old line cook, Sam, who I absolutely couldn't let know I was high.

We made eye contact, and as I looked at Sam, I said,

"Nope",

and shut my door.

This didn't bother Sam. He just put on his music and started prepping. I was panicking now. Who else was coming in? I couldn't check the schedule anymore, because it was out in the kitchen with Sam, and I didn't want to revisit that. I had 90 minutes till 2 more staff would come in, but who would they be?

10:30am comes, and I must open the doors. This was not changing. I was no closer to being down from where I was when I first woke up. The bartender, JB, who had been with me for the last 13 years walked in. He was a Hip Hop DJ in his outside life, and again, surely, he had to know what to do. Before I could even ask, JB knew something was up.

"JB, have you ever had an edible?"

The smile on his face, brimming from ear to ear.

"Never mind!",

I walked to the front door. No one was going to help me.

I came back from opening the front door, and my server had just walked up from downstairs, Kelsey. My savior for this day.

Kelsey was a college senior Political Science major with a good head on her shoulders and she was a sorority girl. I was certain she would make fun of this moment, but not while we were in it, and I have told her thank you for this day, because she deserved it.

“Kels, have you ever had an edible?”, I asked.

“Yeah, they aren’t great. I had one and it lasted for like 22 hours. Horrible. Why do you ask?”,

She hadn’t put it together.

Taking a step back, Kelsey looked at me, “Are you high?”

“I think so?”,

I told her and explained how I got to this point so far.

“Ok, go sit on the bench, I got the lunch rush today.”, she said.

I don’t really remember how fast time, went. I know that it was some sort of beer ordering day, because many reps came in to take my orders, although I don’t remember giving them. Some of them brought pineapple upside down cake, and ice cream, because I had previously said I had never had it. This is a point of contention as to how good it was according to Kelsey, because I was calling her over from the dining room to try some on my bench with me, and we were busy. If you happen to come in that day and remember some slothy looking guy eating from a gallon ice cream container with a huge piece of pineapple upside down cake, I am sorry for your experience, it wasn’t my best effort.

My wife called to check on me around 2pm, shortly after she woke up.

“How are you doing?”, she asked.

“Well, I know what eating an edible is like now.”,

I told her. I was finally coming down and was confident I could wait for Rowan at the bus stop with the other parents and hold a reasonably normal conversation.

Edibles are bad news, and I am certain that if I never have one the rest of my life, it will be just fine with me.

If you are reading this, thanks again, Kels.

## We are the Champions

*"Day 15...*

*Frito Lay is sending me coupons for the bag of flamin' hot popcorn they shorted me in my popcorn tin... is there such a thing as double coupon day anymore?... If so, I am using these to the fullest...*

*I really want tacos... I have all the ingredients to make them... but it always tastes better when someone else makes them...*

*I haven't had 1 Oreo this quarantine... my neighbors have been good to my wife this time around...*

*Insomnia cookies have "Buy 1 get 1 free" dozen cookies... that seems too good to pass up..."*

*"Day 16...*

*I have reached the point where I am trying to find a show to binge... I have found that show...*

*"We are the Champions" on Netflix... this show is an episodic documentary on oddball competitions... 6 episodes featuring cheese chasing, hot pepper eaters, fantasy hair styles, yo-yo's, dog dancing, and frog jumpers, narrated by Rainn Wilson... I love this...*

*We did start watching Christmas cookie bake offs on Food Network... my wife has been inspired... today, she is getting ingredients ready... I better finish what's in the freezer... we have to make room..."*

*"Day 17...*

*Rowan and I continue our game of catch with the football... Until today, his record for consecutive catches was 6... he broke that record... and I screamed 31 FLAVORS, as he caught his 31st consecutive catch...*

*Rowan said, "31 catches, Dad, not 31 flavors." ...*

*I don't think I should tell him that 31 flavors is in reference to ice cream... but this says a lot about my mindset, and that my son thinks I am an idiot that doesn't know what a catch is...*

*It's National Cookie Day... I am eating the cookies from the freezer to make room for all the cookies that my wife is baking today..."*

*"Day 18...*

*I have started to eat the cookies in the freezer at warp speed because my wife is making cookies and we don't have storage for them...*

*I have watched so much "Christmas Sugar Rush" on Netflix that I think the combo of the two have given me diabetes... don't worry... it's a joke... I am pretty sure I am immune from diabetes... I have tried...*

*Mulan, the live action movie was released on Disney+... it was a pretty great movie..."*

*"Day 19...*

*My wife spent 9 hours making Christmas cookies yesterday... towards the end, she finally asked me to help decorate... so I did... but I don't come quietly...*

*I started to sing Rick Astley... I "Rick-rolled" my wife... or so I thought...*

*My wife likes to sing duets... so she jumped in... when the part hits, "NEVER GONNA GIVE! NEVER GONNA GIVE! NEVER GONNA GIVE!", there she was, in all her splendor... this is why we are married...*

*Rowan just told me cows have 4 stomachs as he is finishing a bowl of salt and vinegar chips...*

*Episode 5 of "We are the Champions" is about Olympic-style competition Dog Dancing... The Russian team is unstoppable..."*

*"Day 20...*

*Shakespeare's is closed from dine-in for another 2 weeks... and probably counting... so I have officially started sweatpants season!*

*"We are the Champions" season finale is frog jumping... One of the guys who enters every year says he will beat the average contestant every time... I watched it... I don't think he has a point...*

*I did find out the cheese chasing competition was cancelled this year due to COVID...that was disappointing...*

*Turns out when you freeze cookies, if you aren't careful, they break into tiny pieces that would be rude to share with others... I am going to have to eat them...*

*My mother has never paid a bill online or by phone in her life... I helped her do it today... and she absolutely doesn't believe it went through... and she looks at me like I had messed it up... but if my sister had done it, it would have worked... usually I like playing dumb because it gets me out of household chores... but my sister isn't better than me, although, you can't ask my mother this..."*

I didn't realize how much time I had spent investing genuine care into the show, "We are the Champions", but this is proof enough. Mindless fun, and educational that these actual events are real and take place. I won't break down each episode here, but I will give insight further into my favorite competitions from it. The very first episode about cheese chasing grabs you if you have any interest in comedy that results in an actual competition. I decided to research the event, for those of you that may ever want to enter.

"The Cooper's Hill Cheese-Rolling and Wake" is an annual event held on Spring Bank Holiday at Cooper's Hill near Gloucester in England. 25 Participants race down a 200-yard-long hill, chasing a double Gloucester cheese wheel. There are 2 races, broken up between men and women. Reading this doesn't do it justice, but after the show "We are the Champions" aired, the event was re-established after a 3-year hiatus. In 2022 the returning competition was won by an American woman, Abby Lampe, from North

Carolina who trained by running down hills near her home and studying hours and hours of film. She was the first American to ever win the competition and did so in an impressive 15 second run. I have no idea if this was the world record, but good for her. The Governor of North Carolina even tweeted after her victory, "This is quite an accomplishment. Congrats Abby Lampe on becoming the cheese-rolling champion of the world."

Episode 2 is about chili pepper eating. The World Championship of Chili Pepper Eating Tournament is hosted in Fort Mill, South Carolina, the home of "Smokin" Ed Currie, arguably the world's foremost authority on peppers and the inventor of the world's hottest chili pepper, the Carolina Reaper. As you watch the episode, it becomes increasingly insane to consume the peppers presented, and one woman looks as if she is in labor with sweat and makeup streaming down her face.

If you google chili pepper eating champion, many names come up, and may different tournaments and leagues are presented, so there apparently isn't one official tournament considered the best of the best. I hope this changes, I would like to know who the world champion is without debate.

The season finale of the show is about frog jumping. Angels Camp, California is the world championship of frog jumping and is taken very seriously. The episode focuses on two rival families that have been competing against each other for decades, the Kitchell and the Gustine family. The Gustine family has it down to a science according to the episode, by handpicking frogs from the same river, which they keep secret, for over 60 years and then running the frogs through extensive training at "Croaker College" before settling on one frog for each family member they will rely on to win the year's competition. There are 50 contestants each year, and it is not limited to the two families, but it seems they are the bulk of the competitors. The episode does focus on beating a legendary frog from decades past and the drama of possibly doing so. The winner gets a large trophy, $700, and a metal tile with their name embedded in the sidewalk along the "Hop of Fame". The winning frog is then returned to the secret river in hopes it will breed an even better frog next year.

You can't make this stuff up.

## Tackle Boxes & Mom's Bills

*"Day 21...*

*I couldn't sleep so I got up at 3am... peanut brittle is a national treasure... it should be consumed year-round and not just during the holiday season... at least that's what happens in our household...*

*I ran out of episodes of "We are the Champions." ...*

*I tried to take a nap, but that is when my 8-year-old decided it was a good idea to whisper, "Dad, are you sleeping?" ...*

*I guess not...*

*My wife has been exercising while I eat my weight in sugar... she then shows me the squat kicks she was doing which comes dangerously close to my face... I don't think I deserve such treatment...*

*Is it me, or do all mothers while visiting their children tell them how they would decorate/organize the house if they lived there?*

*There is a show on HGTV where a divorced couple buys houses to fix them up and flip them... my wife loves what they do to the houses... I am there for the passive-aggressive insults...*

*I work this Friday for the first time in over 2 weeks...*

*This pandemic has reminded me that it isn't just my job I am out of, but my skill set is in the toilet too..."*

*"Day 22...*

*My wife volunteered all day at her church to help monitor kids who have online school, and their parents are working... this leaves me with our son to teach... our son has confirmed he thinks I'm an idiot...*

*My wife left at 9am... my son came out at 9:05am saying he was done till 10:55am... I checked... his teacher was still teaching... his break would be from 9:55am-10:05am... and then right at it until 12:10pm... I guess I am not so dumb... he is grounded though...*

*My mother is staying through the holidays unexpectedly and has really started to worry about paying her bills... she brings it up every day... so I decided to pay them today online... all of her bills are paid in full... there is nothing to pay... but she insists I pay them... but they don't exist... so I might be the idiot my son thinks I am...*

*Root beer must have loads of sugar in it, and is a terrible replacement for water in your child's lunch...*

*My mother remembered she had to pay her tax bill... I found it... it's due... In February... it's late November... But she won't sleep knowing she owes something... I can't pay it online... so she called my sister... it's paid for now...*

*Little by little, I am coming to terms with my lack of intelligence..."*

*"Day 23…*

*My mother got all of her bills taken care of… but not as you may think… she spoke to my sister… she wrote a check to my sister and had me mail the check to my sister… I think my argument for the favorite child has taken a significant shift in my sister's favor… I'm still better off than my brother though…*

*I drink an antioxidant sparkling water called Bubbl'r. I think they may be paying attention to me, because they posted a cookie recipe today on Facebook…*

*My wife and I were talking about drug-related offenses being reversed in Michigan… Rowan asked me what drugs were and what they did… I tried to keep it simple by saying sometimes you can't control yourself when you are on drugs… he paused… then said, "I can't control myself sometimes anyway." I don't know what to do with this comment and I may have led him down a dark hole… this is why my wife handles these things…*

*Cyberpunk 2077 came out today… it has a strategy guide… a very large strategy guide… it intimidated me, so now I may have to skip it…*

*Tomorrow, I work for the first time since before Thanksgiving, and I can't wait…"*

*"Day 24…*

*Cyberpunk is a really mature video game for smart people… I think I may stick with my overweight plumber who eats mushrooms and turns in to a raccoon from time to time…*

*My mother was hungry and way past her lunch time... I got my wife on the phone to see if she would like anything... between the two of them apparently, they decided on splitting a chicken salad AND a chicken salad sandwich they wanted me to pick up...*

*I only got the chicken salad... my mother continues to mumble under her breath asking,*

*"Where's my sandwich?"*

*I went to Mackenzie's today to get Scottish Struan bread and they were sold out... that's awesome! Plus, I had to settle on getting frosted sugar cookies... My wife said I didn't need them... but I am an adult...*

*I get to make nachos starting in about an hour! I really miss my job!"*

When the first shut down hit the restaurants, many in the industry who were known for dine-in service started doing carry-out with special dinner boxes. It was smaller portions of some of the favorite dishes made by the restaurant. Scott doesn't usually eat from many restaurants other than our place, and home-made meals are his go-to. We were doing great with our nacho carry-out because we weren't open every day, and it was a special event for a moment, to do so. Then with the second lock down we were doing carry out every Thursday-Saturday for wings, pizza, and nachos. We were slower and weren't making enough to justify being open. Then it hit me, that we should also do a dinner box for carry-out.

I took one of our pizza boxes, made a flat nacho surrounded by pretzel bites and beer cheese, and a quesadilla. Then I decided on a second box with a pizza, surrounded by 3 chicken tenders, 3 potato skins, and 3 cheese sticks. I affectionately called it "Shakespeare's Tackle Box" relating to the Rod and Reel company of its past. Scott didn't understand it. He hated it. He also thought that people wouldn't like it, and it would be a waste of time and money. We have never fought much in 19 years, and I can count on 1 hand where we yelled at each other, but this was one of those times. We were tired. The year had taken its toll on us, and I think having not been in a position in a very long time where our future was uncertain didn't help things. I knew we didn't need to do carry-out with the small amount of traffic we were generating unless we tried something new. Scott doesn't like change, but he stepped back, calmed down, and agreed to give it a try. We announced our tackle boxes and immediately, we were busy. With lines of cars around our building and parking lot. This worked and continued to work for the entire duration of the shutdown, being busy each day we were open. We kept the tackle boxes around a couple months after lifting the lockdown because traffic was still slow for dine in. It isn't something we do today, but we may bring them back for special events someday. Never say never.

My mother has passed down an anxiety to me of not living up to obligations. This may be the reason we have great credit scores, but what it also does is make us stay awake if we think we owe someone anything. I did pay her bills from her accounts while she stayed with us, but in some instances, we had paid them so early, that when she got home, the banks and creditors recognized them as 2 payments in one month and not 2 separate months of payments. She got a late fee for the next month for not having paid. I don't know exactly how the customer service rep from her cable company handled it when she called to explain this, but I am certain they deserve an apology. My mother is a tough lady, and I am sure if you cross her, therapy would be recommended to get over her reaction.

I have explained to my mother that waiting to pay your bills so that these things won't happen is better than being premature, but I believe my mother likes to hear "I told you so" from me. This way, she can say things like "This never happen when Kathy (my sister) takes care of it". I believe now that my sister tells my mother that things are paid for, but they aren't. My sister is just smart enough to do it in a timely fashion. I learn something new every day.

## Home Depot Sucks

*"Day 25...*

*My future brother-in-law made cheesy potatoes and 2 different kinds of Mac n Cheese for lunch... he also made smoked pulled pork... If my sister-in-law messes this up, I'm going to kill her... He's blood to me now...*

*I left my mother home to take care of our kittens, who have a tendency to climb all of our curtains and Christmas tree... we left her with the spray bottle, that works very well at this... 30 minutes in, my mother calls to tell us the water bottle was empty, and she has surrendered... I hope we have curtains left when we get home...*

*There are peanut butter balls, cookies, apple crisp, and no bake cookies here... I think I saw a brownie tray... the kids are sneaking them... when they get in trouble, I sneak some while they are getting yelled at... at the end of the day, they will take the blame... I am a genius...*

*I forgot to wear sweatpants... these jeans aren't very comfortable..."*

*"Day 26...*

*Christmas with my wife's family... my sister-in-law gave all the siblings a tin canister of chocolate covered potato chips... except for me... she gave me... 3 CANS! I don't have to tell you how this ends... but I will...*

*I ate one can already, by myself... and I had 2 more left... but I was deciding I want to limit my grotesque appearance for the sake of my marriage... so I shared with my friends... because my wife still has a can... and I'm going to eat that... because she stole the winter socks I got from my mother-in-law...*

*My father-in-law got me a blanket... a blanket that says, "This is my Hallmark Christmas Movie Blanket". It will go great with my Hallmark Christmas Movie Socks... Have I already mentioned my wife could have married better?*

*My 8-year-old can live on hamburgers... but plain hamburgers with just ketchup... it amazes me how many times I have ordered him one and they put cheese on it... so his lunch today was fries... I'm a great parent...*

*The Lions are going to win today, I can feel it."*

*"Day 27...*

*I'm a pretty good cook... I wrote the menu at the pub... and I am the responsible party for the Shakespeare's nacho recipe... yep, that was me... however, whenever my mother watches me cook with a confused look on her face I second guess even the things I have made for years... It's amazing how a 4'9" lady has such Jedi mind control... I was making stew... she decided she was taking over making the stew after watching me...*

*My kittens have become immune to water bottles and anti-scratch spray... soon, we will have no curtains...*

*My wife left me alone again to teach our son... she has more faith in my abilities than she should, or she is just fine with our son being illiterate...*

*I decided to exercise today... but I think I may have changed my mind... I was wrong, the Lions lost..."*

*"Day 28...*

*I have always appreciated that my 8-year-old doesn't have it in himself to question if we have presents hidden around the house... I am not sure if he believes in Santa... I am not sure if he thinks we buy presents... all I know is, the stack of Amazon packages in our bedroom in plain view hasn't crossed his mind as being fishy...*

*My wife and I went shopping today for matching pajama sets for the family... my wife was in the shopping mood... a gym membership, a trampoline, and a winter jacket later, I realize I didn't get any pajamas...*

*My mother has reminded me each day how she has been craving a chicken salad sandwich... all because I didn't get her one the other day...*

*I haven't eaten sugar for 2 days... but I have prepared to eat sugar in the future, because I am a planner...*

*My mother-in-law bought my 8-year-old an indoor hover soccer game... I am tired just looking at it... yet I am sure I am going to be the permanent opponent...*

*We are going downtown to see the city Christmas lights..."*

My in-laws are great people. They divorced before I ever met my wife, but not before having spent 17 years together and 5 children. My mother-in-law is stronger than she gives herself credit for, and a true mother in every sense of the word. Compassionate, kind, but strong and assertive when she needs to be. I was told she wasn't always this way, but like my wife, she has evolved over time to be something she should be very proud of. In her 50's she became a Border Patrol Officer. Going through an intense training with people half her age and completing it. She did this job for the rest of her working years until she finally, and recently, retired. She often said I was the daughter she never had at Thanksgiving because I would go Black Friday shopping with her when her own daughters wouldn't. It's a title I am still proud to have.

My father-in-law is a tolerant, headstrong, "Man's man". He spent leisure time hunting and fishing. Get him in a room with anyone and he can have a conversation with them, controlling the room with ease. It's a skill to be such a chameleon, adapting to your environment no matter the crowd. I have seen him in rooms with the very rich, skilled and powerful businessmen, and in other rooms with blue-collared, callused hands middle class workhorses. He can relate to both, and neither ever act as if he is out of place. It's funny because he really doesn't have all that much in common with me but treats me with all the respect in the world and tries to relate to my interests. The man bought me a "Hallmark Christmas movie" blanket. I am not sure he has ever seen one of these horrible movies. While those are on, he is more than likely Ice fishing somewhere or in a tree, hunting deer.

The holidays for Angela and I are the most traveling we do all year. We live in Western Michigan and both of our families live on the East side. We spend 1 weekend with her mother, 1 weekend with her father, and Christmas Eve with my mother. Christmas at Angela's has always been one of my favorite times, because my brother-in-law, Bob, and I always find a way to entertain each other.

One year, while doing the gift exchange at my father-in-law's house, Angela and I had gotten him a gift certificate to Lowe's Home Improvement. My father-in-law, also named Bob, usually opened his presents, standing in front of the family and gave some sort of acceptance thank you speech. As he opened his Lowe's gift certificate, he started,

"Lowe's! Thank you. Lowe's is the best. I rarely go to any other Home Improvement store. We don't have Menard's close, and don't get me started on Home Depot."

My brother-in-law, Bob, interrupted,

"What's wrong with Home Depot?"

My father-in-law continued,

"It's overpriced. I went there to get insulation..."

As my father-in-law was telling his story about the negatives of Home Depot, my brother-in-law leaned over and whispered to me,

"I got him a Home Depot gift card."

This information was like taking a kid to the toy store and giving him an unlimited budget. I was ultra-focused on all the points of the story from this point, as my father-in-law continued his diatribe,

"Then I needed 2x4's and wouldn't you know it, they are like $1.50 more a stud. That's highway robbery. I just don't see the point to go there anymore."

He was finished with his rant, put our card down, and my brother-in-law was fast to act,

"Here, this is from Kathy (my sister-in-law) and I."

My father-in-law opened the card slowly. I was on the edge of my seat waiting for his expression of "foot in mouth syndrome" about to happen. Here it was, he opened the envelope and there was a Home Depot Gift Card. Without missing a beat, my father-in-law acted as if he didn't just go on a Home Depot rant,

"You know what I can use this for?",

he started, ready to answer his own question.

"NO!",

my Brother-in-law started,

"Home Depot sucks! You can get gum! Use it for Gum!"

Not to be outdone, I had to add to the chaos,

"Yeah, screw Home Depot, you have $50 there, Dad, you can buy at least 3 packs of gum. If it were Lowe's, you could at least triple that total."

My father-in-Law just let us finish, get it all out of our system. What was he going to do? He knew he went on his rant, without intentionally insulting anyone, but sometimes it just happens.

"You think nails are economically adjusted to the proper price there, Dad?",

my Brother-in-law continued.

"Shingles! I bet they have a good price on shingles!",

I added.

This became a running joke each Christmas, and a story to tell anyone new to come into our lives. For the record, Home Depot doesn't suck, and I find them to be very competitively priced for a Home Improvement store (legality purposes of slander).

## Rowan buys Presents

*"Day 29...*

*My wife has used the time off work to help children with their virtual schooling... I just texted her to ask if the cashmere lined yoga pants I found for her are ok if they come after Christmas?... We both have priorities, but they are not the same...*

*My mother finally got her chicken salad sandwich...*

*Microwave pancakes are a life saver in this house... 2 minutes and my 8-year-old thinks I am royalty...*

*My mother argued with me that the stew I made had enough sauce, even though I said it didn't... today I reheated it and she said it doesn't have enough sauce... I am not going to argue with her on this now...*

*Hover soccer resulted in a laceration on my fingertip like a paper cut... we had to call the game due to injury... safety first...*

*We didn't see the Christmas lights downtown yesterday because most of the shops were closed so we are going today... I didn't think this through... at least the matching family pajamas will be purchased locally...*

*I think I am going to try something new and make my own cookies today..."*

*"Day 30…*

*I wake up every day with the intent to better myself… however… the day started at 2am when the blind chihuahua decided we should not sleep, and a cat named Bob blamed me for the cold weather, keeping him from staying out…*

*So instead, I made huge boxes of fried, high calorie, high carb food to sell at the pub and my breakfast was cheese sticks and some sort of streusel…*

*My 8-year-old knows I'm not really working right now so he made me a Christmas card and insisted I open it… it had $1 in it… to help pay the bills... it's sad and funny, and damn it all, my kid makes me so proud to be his father…*

*My mother-in-law bought my 8-year-old a dinosaur egg that you soak in water, and it hatches… IN 72 HOURS! This is my favorite gift and is pure torture for him to wait…*

*I still fit in my khaki pants… so I can eat more cookies…*

*Reese's make Potato Chip peanut butter cups now… new candy is my favorite part of Walmart…*

*I saw the lights downtown last night… I love Candy Cane Lane…"*

*"Day 31…*

*My 8-year-old couldn't wait anymore… he broke up the dinosaur egg, got the dinosaur out, and left it on the counter… almost 3 days… I wish I would have filmed the anticipation leading up to it…*

*Last night at bedtime was the revealing of deep thoughts... Santa can't live forever... it must be generations of him that keep it going... I'll take it...*

*Rowan and I watched "Rudy" for the first time for both of us... what I took from it... Adidas Sambas are the official shoe of Notre Dame football...*

*My wife wanted to watch the movie, "The Holiday" with my mother, who has never seen it... It was $4 to rent and $8 to own... she insisted we rent it to save money... but I know next year she will want to see it again... so when she wasn't looking... anyway, I spent $8...*

*My friends dropped off a plate of cookies last night... there was a variety, but I am partial to sugar cookies... but also, I am chivalrous... so I offered my wife, mother, and son first choice... My first 2 choices were taken... but my wife knew I would want the last sugar cookie, so she chose differently... I married well...*

*Speaking of cookies... I have an interview with the Huffington Post today about the number of cookies I have consumed over the pandemic...*

*Not joking..."*

*"Day 32...*

*Now that the dinosaur has hatched, he will remain on the counter... the excitement of his existence is over...*

*The kittens and Bob the cat, swap each other's food... kitten food is high in calories... Bob is as big as Garfield now... I don't think he could fit out a cat door even if we installed one... guess my 3am wake call is forever...*

*My neighbor brought over a basket of cookies... Some of the items were labeled with Rowan's name on it... how sad is it that I have given the impression I wouldn't share with my 8-year-old son? I ate his first... out of principle...*

*My sister sent more of my mother's bills... It's Saturday... my mother has been asking me to pay her consumers bill since 7am... I promised her it wasn't going anywhere... apparently there is one more bill still coming...*

*The Huffington Post decided to not do a story on pandemic cookie eating at the moment... they said it will be postponed until January...*

*I can't really work until January 15th anyway... that just gives me more time to rack up the cookie tally..."*

*"Day 33...*

*Today was the last day of the year for Verhage Farms and my wife really wanted Apple cider for mimosas during the winter... so we went... and they had been out of apple cider since mid-November... but we were there... so I hate to waste a trip...*

*My wife bought asparagus... I bought... a red velvet cake roll, 6 donuts, and 6 slices of fudge because it was half off...*

*We then went to Target... my wife wanted a kiss before we went in... then she asked for another... and a third... I wanted to be annoyed but she said, "Act like it's a buffet and you're going back for more!" ... she had me at buffet...*

*While at Target she looked for gifts... I found Oreo candy canes...*

*We then went to World Market because she was on a roll... she looked for more gifts... they had chocolate oranges, Kit Kat flavors I had never seen and Mint Cucumber lemonade... so I bought those too...*

*If there was a show called, "Food Hoarders", I would be on it and in need of an intervention..."*

*"Day 34...*

*Christmas shopping with Rowan... he insisted we go to Home Goods... where he got a "Friends" snow globe for my mother... she has never seen an episode of "Friends" and it had no tag, so we had to wait for a price check... He got my wife a giant thermos for her coffee in the morning... when I say giant, I mean a gallon... he must think she really needs it... everything he picked out was like shopping at a gas station on Christmas morning... I think this is the only person I want to shop with from now on...*

*The "Friends" snow globe is $29.99" ...*

*When you type "Ted" autocorrect changes it to "Yes" ... it's subliminal...*

*My wife found a karaoke rap game to play with our friends... who aren't fans of rap to my knowledge... I kind of* *can't wait to play this... but I didn't buy it... because the snow globe was $29.99... so, I might wait a long time...*

*I drink more Bubbl'r than I eat cookies, which says a lot... however, Bubbl'r is marketed towards health fanatics... they are missing the boat on me..."*

It seemed that Rowan didn't put much thought into his gifts, and I wasn't sure that he was getting them for my wife and my mother because he thought they were cool for him, or he genuinely thought they would love them. My wife read the 5 love languages book, which is a step away from astrology but not necessarily a step up. She likes to tell me that her love language has something to do with communication, I don't really remember, I wasn't paying attention all that well, and that mine is giving and receiving gifts. She nailed that one. I love to give people gifts. I love to get gifts. I have always overdone Christmas and birthdays because there is a rush of Euphoria when someone you care about opens something they really wanted and now have. When I was a kid, I thought my mother had it terrible, because she would get maybe one gift from us, and then buy all of us at least 10 gifts each. Now that I am a parent, I see that she had it pretty good.

We had to wait for Christmas morning to open the gifts from Rowan, which I am jumping ahead for this round of gifts because it relates to an 8-year-olds thought process. My mother opened her "Friends" snow globe. Immediately not knowing anything about the show, she ignored that aspect, and pronounced,

"Oh, it's a giant coffee cup!"

Excitedly, Rowan proclaimed,

"Yep! I know you love coffee, and this was the biggest coffee cup I had ever seen, and you have snow globes all around your house."

The kid was brilliant. I was so focused on the "Friends" portion of the gift that it didn't dawn on me that it was a cup from "Central Perk" the main coffee house in the show. My mother drank coffee every morning before she would let anyone speak to her. He knew this. Also, when you go to my mother's home, she does have tons of snow globes displayed throughout the holidays. I have been conditioned not to notice as much, since they have been a part of my holidays my entire life, but Rowan noticed. He bought her something that worked with more than one of her personality attributes. I had to see the explanation for my wife's gift, and I couldn't wait.

"Angela, this is your gift from Rowan.",

I handed it to my wife.

She opened her giant gallon thermos. Looking at it with wide eyes, Rowan didn't even let her speak.

"Whenever we have a soccer tournament you like to get coffee, Mom, because it's cold and early. I thought that this would last an entire Saturday of games."

He was right again. He put more thought into these purchases than most adults do. He was practical and generous. I often tell my friends I don't know what goes through Rowan's mind or how he comes to conclusions, but when I find out, it's often magical and sincere. He is one of the best people I know, and I am not sure I had anything to do with it.

## Mackenzie's Bakery

*"Day 35...*

*My sister sent another bill for my mother yesterday... my mother asked me to pay it 11 times since I received this information... I told her that my sister didn't send me the website... I then sent my sister a text, knowing very well she would know I could find the info, but was trying to make her look like the incompetent one... good luck being favorite now, kiss ass...*

*The fudge I bought the other day for Christmas... my mother finished a block and blamed it on my 8-year-old...*

*My mother-in-law bought Rowan a metal detector... I believe these were made as a joke... the sensor goes off, and I dig... I find nothing... the sensor stops going off... seems like a lot of work for a dime anyway...*

*We watched "Merry Christmas Charlie Brown." Rowan keeps saying under his breath, "They hate him." And seems sad... I never looked at it that way before...*

*I gave my wife a face mask I received from a brewery. My 6'5" friend, Patrick Walsh wears the same one... My wife says it's soft and feels like a jockstrap and wonders why Patrick likes wearing a jockstrap on his face... I pointed out that it's weird she knows what a jockstrap feels like... I sleep on the couch half the night with the dog anyway, I might as well just save the trip and start there...*

*My wife wants a Fitbit, but she doesn't want it to track her location... she says this as she uses google maps to get us an address around town... I keep thinking I am done ordering cookies, but Insomnia cookies keeps sending me really good deal offers..."*

*"Day 36...*

*Pirouline cookies are better than they get credit for... it's like a straw... that's crunchy... that dips in coffee... that you can skip all these steps and just eat...*

*Nintendo sent me an email with my year in review... it seems that I played over 70 hours of Animal Crossing in April... and not even an hour from July to present day... end of quarantine life destroyed my island... Tom Nook is probably pissed...*

*My 8-year-old sings in the shower... last night it was Feliz Navidad... but it was pronounced "Nameez nummy da" ... it's close... I'll allow it...*

*Milk chocolate potato chips are better than they sound...*

*Listening in on my mother speak to her friends telling them she doesn't have any "wheels" here when she is referring to being without a car... Senior Citizen lingo is amazing!*

*Rowan watches the NFL network like most kids watch cartoons... I hope he is a lifelong sports fan... I love sweatpants Sundays..."*

*"Day 37…*

*6:34am… my mother asked me if there was a way to pay a bill before she's even received it… what kind of anxiety is it called to pay things before they exist? I bet it results in an unbelievable credit score…*

*I have no idea how our toilet seat broke, but I think it has something to do with a certain 8-year-old… anyway, that's what my wife and I are shopping for as a last-minute purchase this holiday season…*

*My mother and Rowan have an amazing dynamic… this morning he was avoiding getting dressed with every excuse he could think of… my mother said, "You have more excuses than Carter has pills" … I think it was in reference to Jimmy Carter, but either way, Rowan said he didn't…*

*With all the Christmas movies I have seen, you may be surprised to know that I have never seen, "White Christmas", or "It's a Wonderful Life."*

*Today was Mackenzie's bakeries last day of business… they sold out of Scottish Struan bread before I ever got a last loaf…*

*Tomorrow, I am going to watch Wonder Woman 1984…"*

*"Day 38...*

*Christmas...*

*Rowan said he wants a tattoo... I told him he could get one of himself, but only taller... he was very confused... and apparently not a Steven Wright fan, because that is one of his classic jokes...*

*My wife called me while driving and she heard a "beeping" noise from my end... excitedly she said, "ARE YOU WORKING OUT?! IS THAT A TREADMILL?!" ... I wasn't... it was the air fryer... they have the same beep...*

*My mother's dog pees on the sidewalk, just before the edge of the grass... what a weird dog thing to do...*

*Rowan got a full football suit for Christmas... he hasn't taken it off and he has been play-calling... and one of the calls is "19-COVID! 19-COVID!"*

*I doubt very much I am taking my pajamas off today... Merry Christmas!"*

*"Day 39...*

*My wife says more quotes from the movie, "Hudson Hawk" than I believe any other human... it is the only movie we whole-heartedly disagree on its greatness or lack thereof... it's horrible... my wife says it's not...*

*I am down to my last tin of sugar cookies... all plates are gone...*

*The Lions lost.... But I am still going to watch next week...*

*My mother made homemade pierogis, so my diet has consisted of large amounts of butter and potato cheese filled dumplings today...*

*My sweatpants are getting tight... time to start exercising..."*

Mackenzie's Bakery was a Kalamazoo Icon for over 40 years. I love bakeries, and when I moved to Kalamazoo from the East side of the State, I was happy to have found them. They made the perfect sugar cookies, fully iced and frosted with just the right amount of sweetness. The downtown location was a block away from Shakespeare's and every Thursday I would go down around 7am and pick up Cashew Chicken Pasta, a couple of the magical sugar cookies, and a loaf of Scottish Struan bread. Struan bread is a soft, multi-grain bread with a slight touch of sweetness and firm, but not crumbly crust. A loaf is football shaped, which is fine because the smaller pieces are great with jam or butter, toasted or not, and the center pieces are great for any kind of cold cut sandwich. Mackenzie's is the only bakery I had ever been to that made Scottish Struan bread and with them in town for 40 years, I thought for sure that I would have it for the rest of my life. Then the pandemic hit, and even Icons close. I tried to make it out the last couple of weeks to get a loaf or two, but there was always a line, and a chalkboard stating they were out of Struan bread. People of Kalamazoo knew what they were losing. Today, Mackenzie's Bakery has been re-established in Vicksburg, a small city not too far from Kalamazoo and sure enough, they have started making Scottish Struan bread again. As Luck would have it, I was able to get it again, and will not take for granted with how great it is.

## The Rollercoaster Xmas

*"Day 40...*

*The amount of Christmas presents I purchased where assembly is required reminds me of how I don't think things through and am not as good a planner as I should be... next year, all boxes must be fully assembled...*

*Wonder Woman 1984 is a heaping pile of trash...*

*My mother was showing me how to make pierogis... but she hated my dough... so she started over and mumbled how she should have done it herself in the first place... I should screw up taking the garbage out from now on...*

*My wife has been doing well following a daily exercise routine and would appreciate if I got the sugary treats out of the house... so today, I finished all of them...*

*Christmas candy is already 50% off at Walmart though...*

*It occurred to me that sweatpants are just pajamas you can wear in public without ridicule..."*

*"Day 41...*

*On my quest to eliminate sugar from the house (for my wife) I thought I had succeeded... I forgot about the gift basket of Kit Kat's and chocolate oranges we received... we no longer have chocolate oranges...*

*I left the house to buy anchors for an obstacle wall mounted course for the kittens... but Bob the cat has gained so much weight, I had to make sure I could secure him if he decides to ninja warrior… Otherwise, he may have trust issues…*

*Billy Idol has an unplugged album and it's amazing… who knew?*

*I think I am good at putting things together, until my wife is watching… I can feel her eyes judging my work and suddenly I am terrible at it… Or, subliminally, I am making it seem that way so that she doesn't ask me to do projects anymore…"*

*"Day 42…*

*My wife asked me what happened to the chocolate oranges… I told her they were gone… she said, "I can't believe you guys ate it all."*

*I didn't correct her… she could have left the word, "guys" out…*

*My 8-year-olds friends came over with a fake cockroach to scare my wife and asked me if I wanted "in" on doing so…*

*I'm a 45-year-old man… of course I wanted "in" …*

*I told her to put it on top of the toilet in our bathroom… and then I waited for over an hour to hear the scream…*

*My 8-year-old couldn't wait… He told her he saw a bug in the bathroom… I tried to teach him patience while pulling such a prank… it's the adult thing to do…*

*I think my eldest son forgot we had Kit Kats… I am going to have to eat them…"*

*"Day 43…*

*I ordered a chicken sandwich today at Turbo Chicken and they have milkshakes… but every time I go, they are out of ice cream… because they are so good… or so I hear… so I texted the owner, who is a friend of mine, and told her she was the new McDonald's with a broken ice cream machine… which she is not, but it wouldn't be a true friendship if I didn't give her a hard time…*

*Suddenly, I got a shake while waiting for my food… the truck for delivery had come during their lunch rush… and I assume the poor guy had to go on the truck and unpack the ice cream to make my shake… working in the industry, that was a dick move on my part… and that guy made the best damn banana shake I have ever had… angry milkshakes are the best!*

*My wife stayed up all night watching some English love story show on Netflix… I fell asleep in the first 20 minutes… it seems like Hallmark has a replacement in our household…*

*I really wish I had ordered 2 banana shakes…"*

*"Day 44…*

*My wife dropped the entire box of Christmas ornaments down the stairs, and they broke…*

*When she told me, my first question was,*

*"Did the pickle ornament break?"*

*I forgot to ask her if she was ok first…*

*Happy New Year's Eve..."*

Angela and I have always tried to get one big surprise gift for our boys on Christmas morning. Something they couldn't have predicted. It started with Alex, who I got a giant ball pit the size of the living room. Then a train table larger than a coffee table, which Rowan later inherited. There was a ride on train one year, which Rowan also later inherited. Each year, I had one project to build overnight so that when they woke up on Christmas morning, it was magical. For a while, Santa got credit for all my hard work, but later in life, they realized it was me, and that was worth the wait. One year, Angela and I bought a K'NEX roller coaster. K'nex was a lot like LEGO, but instead of bricks, it was snap together plastic tubes. This project was a 7 ft. tall giant hill with an additional loop hill that ran on an engine giving it strength to make it through the track and back up to the beginning of the giant hill to start over. To wake up to that working on Christmas morning was beyond my imagination, but I was excited to see the look on Alex's face.

As all kids present, past, and future, the hardest night to fall asleep in the entire year, is the night before Christmas. Alex was 4 or 5 years old, so bedtime was usually 8pm, but on this night, we were lucky if he stopped stirring at 10pm. Angela and I usually put a movie on of some sort until it was silent, then she would keep me company as the construction was underway. At about 10:30pm, I opened the box, to find that there were 1200 pieces! I hadn't thought to look at the box, or the instructions, until I opened it to construct it. If I was lucky, He would sleep in till 6am, which gave me about 7 hours to put 1200 pieces together. I wasn't sure if I could do it!

Like all projects I start, I try and make organization piles, but the time crunch and number of piles was becoming overwhelming. I decided the best approach was to follow step-by-step directions and take it in each moment. Before I knew it, 12:30am hit, and I may have been 10% of the way in. Angela looked at me, kissed me on my forehead, and went to sleep. I had the tv on for noise rather than for viewing and kept working away. Around 4am, real progress was being made, and I was close. It was possible I would be able to make it in time. I got the entire structure up, and had to attach each section together, and hope and pray that the little roller coaster would be able to make its way around the track. As I snapped the last piece in place, and started the engine for the rollercoaster, IT WOULDN'T MOVE!! To control my anger and not breaking up all the progress I had made was extremely difficult. Cooler heads prevailed though, and I refocused. Where was I going wrong? I stretched the structure to separate from the track, giving the rollercoaster more room to change direction. I turned it back on, and it started its climb up the hill! As it reached the top and made its way to the bottom, it got stuck. I just about lost my mind! However, I had to do so in mime-fashion, as not to wake my family, throwing fists in the air. Our first cat, Wicket (God rest her soul) laid on the couch watching, very entertained by my frustration.

More adjustments made, the coaster made its way to different parts of the track, getting stuck at section upon section, until finally, it achieved a perfect run! I had to make sure it was right, so with 10 complete runs without a mistake, I finished it! I kissed the cat, who scurried away, not willing to share my excitement, and pumped my fist and danced in complete silence as I checked the time on the clock. 6am! I did it! I might be able to get some sleep, even an hour, so that Alex never knew I stayed up all night.

I brushed my teeth, and climbed into bed next to my wife, who was sound asleep, and kissed her gently on her forehead. My wife is not the kind of person you can wake up from a deep sleep without some sort of negative reaction, which she never remembers. I didn't care though, a quick slap is fine, I accomplished what I didn't think I could.

At 6:20am, just as I was about to enter a deep sleep, a little boy in his Sonic the Hedgehog pajamas came over to my side of the bed, knocked on my forehead with his little hand, and said,

"I think he was here!"

My wife jumped up, which is one of the only days of the year she has this kind of energy to start a day. Admittedly, Angela is not a morning person, and I am, so it cancels out. She picked Alex up, and walked him out to the living room, telling him that Dad would be a second. I didn't need the extra time, I needed to see the face he would make, so I followed.

"A rollercoaster!",

Alex shouted!

My wife appreciates that I am sappy at times, and when I am exhausted, I am most sappy. My eyes filled with tears, as I saw this little human of mine excitedly play with his newfound toy. He opened each present, and over the years, those all became blended as to what they were. You always remember the big ones. My wife whispered to me, after all the presents were open, and the coffee maker was done,

"Why don't you go to bed, I got this."

I kissed her and made my way down the hall, feeling accomplished and full of pride. The last sentence I heard from my eldest son's mouth was,

"Santa thought I was really good this year!"

He certainly did, young man. He certainly did.

## Capitol Raid & Cobra Kai

*"Day 45...*

*Rowan made it to see the ball drop by the power of root beer floats... My superpower of sugar and insomnia has been passed to the next generation...*

*My wife watched me play video games for the first time in a decade and made a reference to how I was killing all the trees and shrubs and how I should try and fold the blankets in the market... she is not a video game person...*

*Rowan told me Obama is playing Notre Dame today and he doesn't know who to root for... I want to tell him it's Alabama, but I like his idea better... I'll take Obama with the spread... he was the POTUS after all...*

*Cobra Kai came out today... I want it to last longer than it will, so I don't know if binge watching is such a good idea..."*

*"Day 46...*

*My wife and I started Cobra Kai season 3 last night at 9pm, right after Rowan went to bed... At 2am, we didn't have any more episodes of Cobra Kai... now we must wait a year... at least... for more Cobra Kai...*

*The sentence, "He/she has to go to bed" is a mother's way of coping with an overactive 8-year-old... this sentence was spoken at 4:45pm...*

*If you have a child who eats more than 3 different meals without complaint, you are an over-achieving parent...*

*Quick tip... leather furniture is the worst if you love the idea of having a kitten... I really wish they would turn a lot of 80's movies into shows like Cobra Kai..."*

*"Day 47...*

*ESPN has the cornhole championships on right now sponsored by Johnsonville Brats... their slogan is You can't spell SaUSAage without the USA." I love this so much...*

*I introduced Rowan to the Sly Cooper game series... There are 4 of them... he loves watching me play and was super impressed I finished the first 3... I got to the last guy and while I was busy, Rowan decided to play and beat him... he now walks around the house telling me I only finished 3 of the 4 games... talking trash to your father should be designated as an age of legality... and 8 isn't that age...*

*The Lions last game of the season is today... any my wife wants to go sledding... the game is meaningless, so I don't have a proper argument to stay home... plus it's considered exercise and I have eaten a lot of cookies this past couple of months...*

*Remember when my wife told me to rent "The Holiday" instead of buying it? It's FREE on Peacock now...*

*I just can't win today...."*

*"Day 48…*

*My 8-year-old returned to in-person learning this morning, packed with shoes, a snowsuit, 2 masks, a backpack, lunchbox, and water bottle… he returned wearing a snow suit, and a loaner mask…*

*He said someone stole the rest…*

*I had the house to myself and planned on exercising… but instead I got much further in "Immortals: Fenyx Rising" … the Greek Gods needed my help… I am wearing workout clothes though… so it could still happen at any second…*

*His teacher emailed… he forgot his stuff at school… no thief in these parts…*

*Our dog is completely blind and doesn't react to the cats jumping out at her… I feel like she won because of the lack of reaction…*

*I can't wait to go back to work…"*

*"Day 49…*

*Rowan woke up complaining about how the hairbrush hurts his head… this sparked my wife to do a song parody of Huey Lewis's timeless classic, "I Want a New Drug" but instead, "I Want a New Brush" … just another example of how I married well…*

*When I make Rowan eat oatmeal in the morning, I try and hide chocolate chips at the bottom… but he digs them out and eats them first… then he's suddenly full… the kid already outsmarted me…*

*I went to Turbo Chicken again today... the guy who makes the shakes asked me what flavor of the week I would like next week... he put me on the spot, and I said I would leave it to the experts, but I meant to say Oreo....*

*My mother went home but they are still sending her mail here... and the hearing aid batteries she ordered I had to overnight to her because they were expensive... it cost me $40... I asked her how much it would have been to go get new ones... $25... at least all her bills are paid..."*

*"Day 50...*

*My son has been fighting and picked on by a classmate and I told him to say, "I don't want to fight with you, what can we do different?"*

*He didn't want to say it, but he did... and the other student said, "I don't want to fight with you anymore either."*

*For once, I can take credit for giving good adult advice...*

*Then the United States Capitol got raided and I thought,*

*"I don't want to fight with you anymore, what can we do different?"*

On January 6th, 2021, thousands of Americans gathered in Washington D.C. to storm the Capitol in supposed support of former President Donald Trump. COVID-19 significantly affected the conduct of the 2020 Presidential election. Early voting periods were extended and a loosening or elimination of requirements for obtaining or casting absentee (mail-in) ballots, which millions of Americans used in place of in-person voting because it was believed to be medically safer during this time in our history. Due to the changes in voting options, the Trump campaign filed lawsuits alleging that the changes undermined the constitutional authority of state legislatures to make election law or that it was inviting individual voter fraud. Nearly all the suits were dismissed or withdrawn. Amid all these lawsuits, President Trump claimed the Democratic party was plotting to "rig" the election through voter fraud by forgery, altering, or discarding absentee ballots.

There have been many conspiracy theories on both political sides of how the election went down and was won or lost. Some people believe that the capitol was raided by Democratic "plants" rather than Republican Trump supporters to cause chaos within the media coverage. Others believe the election was truly rigged and hypothesize with evidence why.

As a bar owner, one of the golden rules is never to engage in talks of religion or politics within the pub walls. It is always good to remain neutral and even better to keep your own beliefs close to your vest. We live in a democracy allowing us to vote for our chosen leaders. It's what this country was built on, and why I tell my sons it's great to be an American. On this day though, with all the media coverage of our country in uproar, it was hard to explain to my 8-year-old that this isn't the normal response to a Presidential election.

I have no idea if the election was rigged, or if it was truly legit. I have no idea if the riot at the capitol was a conspiracy theorists dream or if it truly was Republicans in support of overthrowing a system, they believed lied to them. What I do know is I don't want Rowan to live in a society that decides that the democracy they live in isn't in our best interest. I want him to believe that ultimately, people want what's best for all, not what's best for some. It's hard to teach or preach what I thought our parents instilled in us when the negative alternative is plastered in front of us on every screen. Donald Trump may run for President again, and if he doesn't there will be a Republican candidate, without question. I just hope my sons know to vote for human decency and the betterment of all people rather than a select few. You can interpret that from either side as being an attack on Republicans or Democrats. I hope that you will see it as a necessity for change, which we absolutely need.

It would have been easier to talk about my love for "Cobra Kai" during this time, but it's not every day that you see a dark part of history occur before your eyes. To summarize those days of episodic joy though, "Cobra Kai" is the best sequel to the original "Karate Kid" of all the sequels. Lastly, and I will debate this with anyone; Johnny Lawrence was the good guy, when you see it from his eyes.

## Presidential & Turbo Chicken

*"Day 51...*

*When on hold with a customer service line, the best way to make the wait go faster is to eat something crunchy or start a conversation with your wife... you will never finish eating whatever bite you were risk-taking, and your wife hates being ignored... this is full proof...*

*I strained my back lifting chicken wing boxes, and my wife thinks I should take a bath... I have a problem sitting in water that doesn't filter... or have enough chemicals to make my eyes burn... so I will complain instead... this is what it's like being married to me...*

*My wife buys pet food whose slogan is, "The proof is in the poop.", I assume this is referring to healthy stool, but I really just wish the kittens would light a match...*

*We are cleaning our house, and my wife received a gift from my father-in-law of a dragon eating an ice cream cone statuette... my wife isn't known to like dragons... so I don't know if it's symbolic of something, but it's my favorite piece of "art" in the house now...*

*I think I am going to put it on display at the pub..."*

*"Day 52...*

*There is a new show on Netflix called, "The History of Swear Words" ... I want my wife to watch it... if you ask my 8-year-old, she has a swearing problem... and she can learn the origins of what she partakes in so very often... history is a good thing...*

*Her swearing can be out of control, but she is married to me, so I understand...*

*Rowan spent the day in pajamas and when I asked him to get changed into real clothes for the day, he asked what the difference is between his pajamas and my sweatpants?...*

*He has a point..."*

*"Day 53...*

*My 8-year-old woke me up at 6:30am... I asked him to go play in his room because it was Saturday... 15 minutes later, he was back... and then he told my wife what time it was, and she yelled, "Be Quiet!" ...*

*I don't know how many times between the two of us we have yelled "BE QUIET!", but I assume we are giving the wrong message here...*

*My son is determined to convince me that electric guitar is "way cooler" than acoustic guitar... also, he doesn't understand why Van Halen's "Jump" keeps telling people to "Jump" ...*

*"Why do they keep saying Jump?"*

*"What are they Jumping for?"*

*I had never thought of the answer, and I have no idea what they are doing in this song...*

*It is one of the two days of the week at the moment that I contribute to the economy with carry-out Tackle Boxes of chicken wings… I always smell like them when I get home…"*

*"Day 54…*

*Rowan has been playing Madden on the Xbox on exhibition mode as the Lions and keeps winning… he said, "The Lions never play like this." …*

*Reese's makes snack cakes now… Oreo has "Brookie" flavor… January is a hard month to start getting back in shape…*

*"Ted Lasso" on Apple TV+ is great…*

*Rowan bet me that Tennessee will beat Baltimore today… if he wins, he gets 5 candy bars… if I win, I get to exercise with his mother… somehow the stakes don't add up…*

*I made chicken in the slow cooker with vegetables… and then I was tagged in a Facebook post by Presidential Brewing Company about a slider box that feeds 4-6 unless your name is "Ted", then it feeds 1… I had to order it… I think maybe we will have leftovers… of something…*

*My wife is going to kill me…"*

*"Day 55…*

*I have held my breath for most of today waiting for the Governor to extend the shutdown… it hasn't happened, so I am going to breathe for now…*

*My wife is a multi-tasker and I know this is why she misplaces things because she is constantly busy... but when she lights a candle in a room we aren't in, I don't know whether to risk blowing it out and getting her mad or risk checking my home insurance... I lean towards the new house...*

*I went to exercise today and one of the kittens decided to climb my back with her sharp little claws... so for my safety, I am done being healthy for the day... it was a good 15 minutes...*

*I have hit the stage where the only masks I have in the car are for my 8-year-old... it still covers everything, but it leaves little to the imagination...*

*The amount of empty water bottles we have throughout the house is infinite... I have never noticed before being semi-unemployed how hydrated our family is..."*

Little known facts about Shakespeare's and particularly, Scott and I; we were going to open a second location at least 2 other times in our history and it just didn't work out for one reason or another. One of those times was in 2018 at a vacant slender piece of bare property in Oshtemo Township, a bordering township of the city of Kalamazoo. The idea for this space was to not only have a pub similar to Shakespeare's, but to create a mini golf course with brewery themed holes and sponsor mini golf tournaments and charity events. We spoke to representatives from Short's, Bells and Founder's Brewing who seemed genuinely interested in the design of signature holes based on their brewing portfolio. With only 18 holes to start, and a possibility for a second course being built in the future, it was almost certain to guarantee a permanent space for beers for any brewery that had their own hole. I was enjoying talking to designers about creating the Short's logo and Soft Parade as an entire hole, or Bell's having a sun for Oberon, a fish for Two-Hearted, and of course, ringing bells. Founder's would have a Woody car complete with surfboard on their hole to represent All Day IPA. We had a lot of ideas in the works, including pricing out the cost of such a venture. It was going great, and then, about 6 months into planning, and deciding whether we would do the space, a little brewery in Portage, MI opened called Presidential Brewing. They were opening in a space that was once occupied by a mini golf course, so you can guess what they had for outdoor entertainment. I read the article, and people who were aware of our planning started to tag me in the Facebook posts sharing the article. This is when I first interacted with Kayleigh Lohse, the First Lady of Presidential Brewing Company.

As a pub owner or manager, it is our nature to be a professional people watcher and to understand cues of human interaction. Kayleigh Lohse was very nice to me on the surface upon hearing that I was looking to do a mini golf course, and now I was shying away from the idea because I would not be the first to get to it in the surrounding area. However, her kindness and words in a social media post were easily seen through as,

"Who the fuck is this guy? He didn't invent mini golf?"

I could tell this lady was tough and smart and not one I truly wanted to have a war of words with now. She was new to our industry and was saying all the right things in a social setting, and she either thought I was attacking her concept, or wasn't sure if I would. I am very aware I did not invent mini golf, but I am also aware that doing the same concept very close to the opening of a new business is a possible nightmare for public perception. We scrapped the idea of it, for now, and went about our business.

It was around January of 2021 when I met Jake Lohse, Kayleigh's husband, the President of Presidential Brewing, at a Kalamazoo Beer Week meeting where I bashed a distributor for ruining the concept and this was the first interaction he would have with me. I asked him about his mini golf course after the meeting and we both exchanged knowledge of how much it cost to produce a proper course. I am assuming that he wasn't sure what I would be like after hearing me rant of how "Hillbilly beer pairings with Hamm's", was a terrible idea for an event to help smaller craft breweries. I think he agreed with me, but his approach may have been different than calling it a "piece of shit" idea.

Jake is mild-mannered, intelligent, and hard to dislike. He's a former computer nerd and loves spread sheets and organizing. My brother would probably love him, because they like to format and find the assumed and probable causes of questions and problems. I believe he is tougher than most assume, because of how he approaches people with a "Let's be friends" aura, he can come off as a push-over. That is far from the case, and as time has gone on, I have found that Jake is one of my favorite people in our industry.

I didn't interact with new breweries much that didn't have a distribution deal because self-distribution is a logistical nightmare for Shakespeare's. Often, the breweries doing this are too small in production to keep up with the volume we are doing and that causes inconsistent availability. Also, they generally don't have a set schedule for delivery, and when a keg is empty, I have to store it until I order from them again, and that could be months if not years. Lastly, if a beer doesn't sell and I get it from the distributor, I don't have to carry it again, they take the empty keg back, and no one is the wiser about it. Telling a brewery their beer didn't do well and they must come get their empties, sucks. It's like the walk of shame after a one-night stand. Presidential was brand new, and were not distributing to anyone at this time, and then the shutdown hit before they even got the first year under their belts. Talk about rough timing.

When the first shutdown occurred, I was in the process of updating our website design. I went on a local Business networking board and asked if anyone could point me in the right direction for designers. On top of all the web designers emailing and messaging me to offer quotes, Kayleigh Lohse reached out and offered to help set me up, with online payments for carry-out and web design. I asked her who she used, and she told me she was willing to help me, on her own, NO COST!

Did I read this lady correctly a year ago when she and I interacted about mini golf? Was she really being sincere?

How did I not know this? My reading of social cues couldn't be that off, could it? I didn't take Kayleigh up on her offer, and did use a professional web designer, but that was a new door being opened to interact with someone else in our industry. There was a local Facebook group we belonged to that during the pandemic, really helped many of us, and through this group, I was able to connect with other local businesses in my industry that we could now bounce ideas off and voice our frustrations to each other. The power of understanding and being able to relate to others is therapeutic in a way that is seldom appreciated. Kayleigh invited me to a private messaging group that also included Kassidy Nieuwenhuis, who with her husband, Mark, owned Kelvin and Co. Urban BBQ and Turbo Chicken. I was very excited for this, because I am a huge fan of pulled pork and brisket, and very frequently ordered Kelvin and Co. meals that feed 3-4 people just for myself. Mark is brilliant at spice and seasoning, and I would put his Carolina BBQ sauce in a challenge against anybody's on earth.

This is when I really started to get to know Kayleigh. Right-brained people are quick witted and intelligent, probably suffer from sort of ADHD, which is a blessing and a curse, and when they are funny, which is most of the time, they are excellent at improvisation. Kayleigh has all of these qualities, but also, the toughness I detected from our initial meeting is very apparent. She isn't afraid to voice her opinion, and in the day and age of social media where a small business owner can lose all that they have for the smallest infractions, or missteps, Kayleigh will defend herself and other businesses without a second thought. That is the loyal side not many get to see. It's quite possible Kayleigh has many friends, but the one's she holds close are probably smaller in number. It's obvious to me that if she trusts you or cares for you, she will fight for you or be by your side helping in the fight.

I knew we were friends, when on my birthday, she filled an entire laundry basket with cookies and dropped it off at my house. Every flavor of Oreo Meijer carried.

I had never met Kassidy before the messaging group we started. Like Kayleigh, she is very quick and intelligent. She's petite in stature but not personality. We have a weird path of similarity and crazy that we had never crossed over it before. Scott and I met working at Buffalo Wild Wings and Kassidy worked there a few years after we had left, for a substantial amount of time with people I had hired. She went to work at the Kalamazoo Beer Exchange, who were my sworn enemies until we made up during the pandemic because I have grown older and less immature with my insecurities. The staff there would come in often. I ate at Kelvin & Company at least twice a week, and she worked register from time to time. Not once did we speak of anything more than how much I owed for my meal, which always seemed like it should have been for a group of people, and not just myself. Then when our little support group started, I got to see how a business in our industry that does more carry-out than dine-in works and was happy to see them succeed when the future was so bleak. Plus, we had this mutual dislike for a start-up business that would use social media to lie about donations to charity and used stock photos of desserts they found on Google, claiming to be their own. It was nice to have a common, yet petty, interest.

People say imitation is a form of flattery, but in my experience, it's just annoying. I could relate to this with Kassidy because this rival business often copied their specials week after week. Shakespeare's had this problem with the beer releases and often fought with the Beer Exchange over it. Today, looking back, we were busier with the Beer Exchange existing much more than when they didn't. I should have thanked him for being my neighbor, and I have told him so since. I also will whole-heartedly admit that the best fried bologna sandwich I have ever eaten, was created at the Kalamazoo Beer Exchange.

I got COVID once, and Kassidy dropped off a milkshake from Turbo Chicken as a "Get Well" gift. Between Kassidy and Kayleigh with gifts of sugar, the pandemic gave me two of my favorite friends today.

Kassidy and Mark moved down the street from me a year or so after we started bitching about industry stuff, and they have two children. Juggling that with being small business owners can be tough. My wife had to do a lot of entertaining our son while I worked, so I get it. Angela and Kassidy have made plans many times to go rollerblading, although to date, it has never happened. I am sure it will. What a small world we live in.

## Moving to Kuai?

*"Day 56...*

*My blind dog insists on leading when we take her out... she runs into the door, the bushes, and the gutters... even at her most vulnerable, she refuses to rely on help... she is an "alpha" in every sense of the term... or she just doesn't trust me after 14 years...*

*Reese's pretzel big cups taste unbelievable and dangerous if you are trying not to eat sugar...*

*Rowan got off the bus today and said he had a good day... all the girls at recess chased him and couldn't catch him, because they were too slow... depending on how you look at it, he is doing this exactly right or completely wrong... either way, the boy has game...*

*Rumor is that we are not going to be able to open for dine-in... but I hate rumors so there is still hope...*

*Speaking of hope... the lottery is over $600 million today... if ever there was a time to buy tickets, it would be today..."*

*"Day 57...*

*I sit and contemplate what other skills I have... I tell Dad jokes... I can write a book... I can be a consultant for an industry that isn't open... I can start a podcast... I can start a blog... some of those skills give you a budget of 500k on House Hunters International...*

*My son has been playing Minecraft with the little girl across the street... they have created a house... their house...*

*apparently, they have married in Minecraft... I need to pay attention more to what is going on in my house... Somehow, I missed the union...*

*I think I want tacos for dinner...*

*There are now 3 girls in my house playing with my son... I don't think I have enough controllers for my Xbox...*

*I don't really want to cook... and there are a lot of Taco places around here..."*

*"Day 58...*

*My wife and I were looking for a new show to watch and saw a preview for "See" on Apple TV+... it's about how all humans are physically blind until these two babies are born with sight and a war starts over the seeing babies... my wife started laughing at this premise, uncontrollably and I asked her what she found so funny? She said, "Warriors who can't see in combat? How? Dammit, I just killed Jimmy!"*

*You might have had to be there for it to be funny, but she has a point... we didn't watch it...*

*Added commentary on this... my wife said she has never wanted to shave a human more than Jason Mimoa, the star of "See" ...*

*I did make tacos yesterday... Rowan said he likes my mother's tacos better... she never made tacos... I did... he didn't believe me so I had to call my mother to clarify... my mother wouldn't validate my story, took claim for them, and then said it doesn't take much to cook tacos anyway...*

*I made sure this lady's bills were paid on time… I guess she raised me though… it cancels out…*

*My wife blamed a bad internet connection during her virtual workout to take a break… it's brilliant… I married a brilliant lady…"*

*"Day 60…*

*I skipped day 59 because of the sudden and unexpected loss of our kitten, Raven… Today, the pub flooded, backed up from city sewage drains…*

*I don't have much left to feel funny about, but I keep hearing the voice in my head to say to my sons,*

*"This is how you lead."*

*I don't feel sorry for myself, I have a good life, I could just use a breather for a moment…"*

In September or October (my wife is better with time lines) we got Rowan his very own kitten. I wanted to name her Steve, but she was a lady, and Stevie wasn't my first choice. Rowan came up with the name, Raven, and it stuck. I called her Ray-Ray for short. She came from a large litter, and she had a sister named, "Stripes" who was one of our favorites but was adopted by another family so we just got Raven. Raven was comfortable in her own skin as a cat is but didn't shy away from Riley or Bob the cat when we brought her home. She was playful, but bored, because she was so much younger than our other animals. That's when we got the call that Stripes was available if we still wanted her. We did. We renamed stripes, Cecelia, CeCe for short. They were inseparable, and mischievous. Raven had claimed Rowan as her owner, which cats often do with one person in a household. Rowan loved her so much. I don't like to cover loss much, but as life lessons go, Raven's curiosity got the best of her just 4 months after we got her, and we couldn't do anything to save her. 2 years later, Rowan still talks about Raven. It's a shame he had to deal with such a traumatic life event, and a little bit of me dies each time he relives it.

The day after Raven past, Scott and I went to the pub to start our weekly carry-out event. Scott had a rough night as well, as his wife had been bitten by a dog in the neighborhood in front of their 5-year-old daughter. As we opened the doors, looked to the bottom of the staircase, we could see inches of standing water before us, and a sewage smell. Years before the pandemic, the city of Kalamazoo had flushed their sewage lines. The piping from the streets didn't have a stop valve that wouldn't allow water to seep into our building and we had 50 thousand gallons of sewage water destroy our entertainment venue. The reconstruction was expensive back then, but we were told that a stop valve was to be installed from the city so this would not take place ever again. That valve was never installed.

Defeated, we looked down at the water, Scott couldn't wait, he was done, and just started walking in it to see the rest of the building. Again, our lower-level entertainment venue was destroyed, with no drainage. Our kitchen had drains and could be saved but it would be weeks before we could be safely operational again. Our time doing carry-out only was done.

We had been through this before, so we knew the proper steps to call and start the process of getting put back together. We did what we could for a Friday afternoon, and then went home to our families. In this moment, I didn't want to work anymore at what I had built with my best friend. I was done.

Angela and I had taken a vacation in 2016 to Hawaii. Everything you hear about it is paradise, and truly deserving of the title. It had been on my mind that we needed a change, and this may be the time to take it. So much so, that I asked Angela to see if she could find jobs as a Speech Pathologist in Hawaii, a career she never pursued but has a degree in. She found 3 jobs available. I had seen a lot of food trucks on the island and debated whether I wanted to go so small for a short amount of time. Anything to change what was happening here.

I wasn't sure what to say to Scott yet, if this would be a reality. I couldn't just leave without helping my friend and partner with the mess we had before us. I knew he would support any decision I made, maybe even deciding it was time for him to do something else too. On top of the pub and insurance responsibilities and the city of Kalamazoo settling with us, there would be an extended period before I could really find answers to what we would do. All of which, could be done remotely if necessary. Angela and I started looking at property and the logistics of leaving Kalamazoo. We had one obstacle we couldn't find a solution we were comfortable with, resulting in the idea of Hawaii to be cancelled. The Blind Chihuahua.

For us to move, Riley would have to be quarantined for 3 weeks in a veterinary hospital when we made it to Kauai, the island we were looking to move to. She would be caged, and we would not be able to come and see her until the time had passed. It was already going to be traumatizing for her to fly on a plane, but she is a good traveler and sleeps the entire time, so we thought she would be ok. However, living in a strange place for 3 weeks without knowing what happened to her family and being blind and diabetic might be too much for her 14-year-old body to handle. Neither of us were willing to put the world's worst dog in a position of life or death, and we truly believed it was. So, we stayed. I don't know if you can credit the blind chihuahua with the existence of Shakespeare's operating today, but it's debatable.

## Teenage Mutant Ninja Turtles

*"Day 61...*

*Probably an unpopular opinion, but I was not fan of the first two episodes of "Wanda Vision" ...*

*My wife plays this game called, "Feel my forehead" ... I can tell you that I am a terrible fake doctor... but I think I say "you're fine" or "you're kind of warm" depending on her facial expression...*

*Brookie Oreos are way too sweet for me... and that is saying something...*

*Why do restaurants on Door Dash change their name? I can't imagine a time where I am happy I ordered and was pleasantly surprised it was from Applebee's...*

*We have 2 Amazon Alexa devices in our home... they are used to settle disputes, answers to Rowan's never-ending list of questions, and cooking timers... in case you needed to know, Andre the Giant once consumed 65 bottles of beer and 8 bottles of wine in a single drinking session... that bar really didn't like their liquor license..."*

*"Day 62...*

*The state of Montana was named for the numerous and surrounding mountains it has... this was the answer to Rowan's question this morning to Alexa...*

*Rowan is a huge Tom Brady fan... he also likes to tell me how Tom Brady is younger than me and that he doesn't understand how Drew Brees is retiring and he's even "more younger" than me...*

*I was told today is "National Michigan Day" ... what exactly does that entail? I bet the roads are destroyed, people say "ope" when in the way of others, and Vernor's cures almost everything...*

*It's just 1 day a year...*

*Throwing out all of my food inventory at the pub was a depressingly necessary activity today... but at least I got exercise going up and down the stairs..."*

*"Day 63...*

*My basement floor is cold... and I have slippers, but they are pushed under the ottoman by the animals... so I may have to lose a toe to frost bite... because moving the ottoman seems like too much effort...*

*Rowan doesn't like tacos from school lunch but today was lucky tray day and if you get the lucky tray, you get a toy... so he said he loved tacos today... but he didn't win the tray... and he came home hungry...*

*Sam's Club has Fanny May chocolate covered s'more trail mix... and as I've stated before, trail mix suggests a healthy lifestyle... it's like I'm exercising at the same time...*

*I let Rowan play 5 minutes of Halo while I took the dog out... now that's all he talks about...*

*My wife gave me a look that made me worried for my safety, much like my mother did as I was growing up...*

*For the life of me, I am not sure what I did, but I'm sure I deserved it… that's called maturity…"*

*"Day 64…*

*Inauguration Day…*

*If the worst thing I see today is a T-shirt that says, "Don't blame me, I didn't vote for him.", I would say this Presidency is off to a good start… either way… I don't care who anyone voted for… that's up to you to live with your choices and decisions…*

*Spectrum TV sent me a notification that House Hunters International's new season starts tonight… season 161… there are 161 seasons of this show… and every food blogger has a better budget than I do… by a lot…*

*Pinterest had a cheeseburger casserole recipe that was low in carbs… it literally is taking Mayo, ketchup, onion, burger, and mustard, mixed up in a casserole dish and covered with cheese… it's a cheeseburger… I don't need to make it in a casserole dish…*

*Rowan has a half day tomorrow… and afterwards, his journey into the Halo Universe will begin…"*

*"Day 65…*

*One of the most irritating things to my wife is hearing someone eat something crunchy… It's kind of a blessing, because that means I can always watch TV while we eat to drown out the crunching sound…*

*Rowan has started making gulping sounds, repeatedly, and I think my wife may be losing years of life from it... which is a shame... because upon my inevitable demise, I would have hoped she would have enjoyed more time from the life insurance payout... because that's how they sell it to you... letting you know your wife will outlive you...*

*I was eating spoons full of peanut butter, but I didn't have a beverage to wash it down and there was almost a choking fatality in the kitchen...*

*Not how I pictured I would go... but Rowan thought I was joking, so I better let up on my physical comedy and sarcasm for my own safety..."*

Years ago, my wife decided that Rowan wasn't mature enough to play online games and we were against the idea of "Fortnite" because of the stories we had heard from other parents about their children's attitudes after playing for an extended period. Being a video game fanatic, I had a lot of games in the house, with all the current systems, that playing a co-op game wouldn't be that big of a deal if he was truly playing games for the actual game's enjoyment. Angela didn't like video games and wouldn't allow Rowan to play during the week while school was in session. He could play on the weekends, but not all weekend long. Just small pockets. Most of the time, because he wasn't playing during the week, he was forgetting about video games entirely on the weekend, and was physically active with his friends on the trampoline or playing soccer, football, riding his bike, etc. It kept him healthy, mentally and physically, so my wife had a point.

One day, while Angela and I were discussing our family budget, and bickering about spending, something we didn't normally do, Rowan was playing video games in the room with us. As we got more heated with our discussion, Rowan started to interrupt. Still not in the moment, we were ignoring him until he spoke a sentence that stopped us, dead silent.

"Dad, I killed all the black guys!"

My wife and I have prided ourselves in raising our children without bias, and choosing equality, and fighting for those who didn't have a voice, and accepting those with different views. If you weren't hurting anyone, we want to be on the side of history that loves one another. To hear this sentence, we were in shock, and a delicate approach from here seemed important.

I could feel my wife staring at me, with the look of, "I told you that video games are a problem, and now look what happened?"

I looked to my son, and slowly asked him, so that he could understand every word,

"What... did... you... just... say...?"

He looked at the screen, never making eye contact with me, so my slow tone didn't impact him the way I thought it might, and he repeated,

"I killed all the black guys!"

My head was about to explode in fear, what have I created?

My wife asked,

"What the hell game is he playing?!"

I hadn't any idea, so I looked at the screen, thinking maybe it was Grand Theft Auto, a game I am not terribly familiar with but rumored to be inappropriate, but I didn't think it was THAT kind of inappropriate.

The game was...

Teenage Mutant Ninja Turtles...

The "Black Guys" were Ninjas...

NINJAS!

Relief came over my entire being. I looked to my wife with a smirk, knowing this was a teaching moment and she could stop blaming video games for all that is wrong with the world. I began to speak,

"Rowan, pause it for a second."

He did, and looked up to me to hear what I had to say,

"Yes, those are black guys because they are wearing black, but we don't refer to them as "Black Guys". They are called "Ninjas".

Looking up to my wife, as if I solved world hunger, I thought that I had fixed the problem, but an unforeseen problem took its place.

Rowan, at this time, had a speech impediment, and the word "Ninja" didn't sound like "Ninja", and the more he tried to say it correctly, the more in sounded like something else, WAY WORSE!

"Right dad "Ninjas", He said, incorrectly, but you can read between the lines.

"NO! NO! NO! LISTEN! Say it like this,

nin JA-JA-JA-JA"

Saying it slowly, he just couldn't make the "J" sound. Over and over again, with so much concentration.

We turned the game off. Put it up, and now tried to explain what he was saying sounded like a word that he could never use. Most kids may push to learn what devious word was and why we were trying to avoid it. Probably using the word in a different public setting to see other's reactions. This is where we have been blessed with Rowan. He accepted my explanation. He didn't ask why, and with a simple shrug said,

"Ok Dad."

And went about playing with his action figures. All of which were not Turtles or Ninjas or Ninja turtles.

Fast-forwarding a few years, Rowan outgrew his speech impediment. Chalk that up to having a wife who majored in Speech Pathology and speech maturity on Rowan's part.

Halo is a game series that I have played since its inception 20 years ago. It's a 1$^{st}$-Peson shooter where you kill an alien antagonist. All great sci-fi stories start and end this way. I was fortunate enough to play with my eldest son, Alex, and now Rowan would be able to play the new games with me as they came out. We played through the entire "Master Chief Collection", and we are patiently waiting for the Co-op campaign for "Halo Infinite" to arrive.

We still haven't played a Ninja Turtles game ever since...

## Our Engagement Story

*"Day 66... The Rowan Post...*

*My 8-year-old rarely wears socks... no matter the temperature or with what he is wearing throughout the house... except at bedtime... he refuses to take his socks off at night because his feet are cold...*

*Someone made a joke to me that Sociopaths wear socks to bed... I hope this isn't the case...*

*Rowan also brought home school lunches for the entire weekend because they were free and giving them away... he said, "I knew we would be hungry, because you love buffets, Dad."*

*He's not wrong... I love buffets, especially in Las Vegas...*

*When Rowan showers at night, he goes to the bathroom after he showers... I know when you have to go, you have to go, but it seems like a counter-productive event cycle...*

*He hates peanut butter but loves Nutella because of the chocolate... but he hates Reese's cups... he loves cheese unless it's melted... he will eat a burger, a taco, hummus, rice, and pizza... carrots and cauliflower because he must... but nothing else...*

*He passes gas when he is excited...*

*And cream soda is his favorite drink, but only if it has espresso in it...*

*My wife won't comment on this post, but she will correct me when she reads some of the facts..."*

*"Day 67...*

*Larry King died at age 87 and my youngest son immediately stated that he was older than my mother... my mother has never forgiven me for telling him her age... because he compares it to antiques...*

*I used Door Dash today for a burger place, but I didn't order any burgers from them... I did order ice cream sandwiches though... and I ordered a lot...*

*Netflix sends me emails to let me know what my 8-year-old is watching, in case I didn't know... First, Netflix thinks I am a terrible parent because I may not know what he is watching... Second, I am glad they don't send my wife emails about my viewing habits...*

*I have never played a Halo game to completion without my eldest son, Alex... it seems this tradition may be passed down to my youngest son...*

*My Aussie friend, Medway, taught me that counterclockwise isn't a term in Australia... they say anti-clockwise...*

*It seems much more defiant..."*

*"Day 68...*

*I ordered cookies from a place called "Underground Cookie Club".*

*First rule of Underground Cookie Club? Don't tell my wife about me ordering from Underground Cookie Club...*

*"Ringfit" for the Nintendo Switch is hard...*

*My Aussie friend asked I could play video games today... I waited my whole life to make adult decisions on my own... it's something else to believe I must ask anyone if I do something... I told him maybe; I have to ask my wife...*

*My wife couldn't remember the name of the makeup company she buys from... I told her it was Roden and Fields... off the top of my head... she married well, I tell her all the time...*

*I have to put new floors in my bathroom... and my wife finds the one floor sample you must order online for more money than I am ever willing to spend... so I am going to play video games... without asking..."*

*"Day 69 (nice)...*

*My 8-year-old says that Batman is the worst superhero, all his friends say so, and they aren't changing their minds... reason number 7158 why he needs to be grounded...*

*I had every intention of eating better today, but breakfast was an ice cream sandwich and lunch was left over pierogis... I'm on a budget...*

*Kentucky Fried Chicken makes their own fire log for your fireplace... now you can have the smell of fast-food kitchen throughout your house... if that doesn't spell romance, I don't know what does...*

*My youngest son and a friend of his were using our home gym and the motivation speech is really good....*

*"You lost 2lbs. of inches."*

*"I weigh 75ft. 5""*

*"Did you see how much I just did? I'm the bomb.com"*

*This motivated me to do some push-ups... I want to be the bomb.com too..."*

*"Day 70...*

*Looking out the window to a winter wonderland, Rowan said, "It must have snowed." It's hard not to call him "Captain Obvious" but then I would have to explain who Captain Obvious is...*

*I have a shopping list consisting of wet dog food, whip cream, and syrup... this isn't the chihuahuas diet, but it would explain the diabetes if it was...*

*She's the worst...*

*I did everything you could possibly do in "Immortals: Fenyx Rising" ... being unemployed for the most part has shown I can rule Mythological stories like a God... I'm halfway there.... I'm Greek...*

*Sledding in my backyard and getting jeans wet is the worst... how on earth did I manage to go through an entire school day when I was younger like this?*

*Hopefully, less than a week away, and I can go back to work, full time..."*

Angela and I have lived in 2 apartments and 2 houses together. I would have never moved out of an apartment, had my wife not been insistent on wanting to own a home. Our little 1200 square foot first home saw 1 cat, 2 dogs, and 1 son raised in it, and 1 son begin his life there. We built a Man Cave basement, complete with draft system which had root beer and Hard Cider on. My wife planted flowers and the infamous "decorative grass mowing" which saw me get cancelled from being allowed to do lawn work was at this home.

We were together for 7 years before we got engaged. I had a rough outlook on the idea of "Forever" and one person is ultimately your soulmate. Life seems very complicated and isn't like you see in a movie. Mine is close though, and I wouldn't trade it in for the world, looking at it today.

In September of 2008, I started thinking of Angela's birthday coming up in November. After 7 years together she had seen enough material presents, some better than others, (I have never lived down the quesadilla maker) and I didn't have any great ideas to surprise her with. My wife had always wanted to go on a spontaneous trip, and there are so many places we had never been, mostly because I had never planned a vacation in our entire relationship. I decided this was the gift, a surprise trip somewhere. My wife likes tropical beaches and active excursions, which would have made more sense to plan. I decided on a hot desert, with all night gambling, in a city that never sleeps. Las Vegas.

I started looking at deals for travel and hotels and sights to see. Take in a few shows if we could. I had always wanted to see the "Blue Man Group", and Angela was in love with the idea of "Cirque Du Soleil". The Vegas strip had all these theme-based hotels like the Venetian with Gondola boat rides, New York, New York with a roller coaster, and Paris Las Vegas with an Eiffel Tower. It was overwhelming to choose, and this is the biggest reason why I don't plan trips. A lot of people get excited about the choices, I get anxiety.

Ultimately, I chose Planet Hollywood because I could get tickets to "Blue Man Group" which was playing in Planet Hollywood an hour after we got off the plane. Las Vegas entertainment tickets are expensive! It makes up for how cheap the room rates are. With my search of these hotels, I ran across a google ad,

"Top Ten places in Las Vegas to propose to your girlfriend."

"Propose?", I thought.

We had been together 7 years, and I planned my life with Angela in it. It was going to be us. There was no "For now" in my mind. I had evolved to never knowing what I was doing the next day, let alone next year, to this is my person forever. It never struck me that was the case until reading this little Google clickbait. I wanted to ask my wife to marry me.

I started shopping for rings, and when you do that, you have all kinds of prices and qualities to research. Anyone who proposes to their significant other wants it to be the best. Magical. I remember sticker shock from a private jeweler, asking a quarter of what I paid for my house and thinking I would never be able to afford it. Then I saw the mall jewelers who had cheap pricing but claimed high quality. I had no idea how to do this, and of all people to give me advice, Jim the plumber led me to the place to buy my wife's ring. This more than made up for him screwing up the urinal install.

I now had the ring, but I had to ask her parents' permission. Yes, we lived together for the past 7 years, and I knew the answer was going to be yes (at least I hoped), but my father-in-law especially is a man who believes in old-fashioned respect, and I owed that to him. I planned on making a 3-hour trip across the state to see him and ask for his permission to marry his oldest daughter, but when I called, he told me he was coming to visit us in 2 weeks. I would ask him then.

Next was my mother-in-law. I was going to call her and go see her now, but as I was doing so, Angela told me,

"Hey, my mom is coming for my birthday for the day."

We were leaving for Vegas the day after her birthday, so I had to subtly get information on what the plan was, as to not disrupt my mother-in-law visiting,

"Oh, that's great! Is she coming for the weekend?"

"No, just the night. Her and Jackie (My brother-in-law, Bob's future ex-wife, and the reason I had to adopt Riley) are coming in for shopping and dinner."

"Fantastic!", I said, knowing that I could ask then. Things were falling into place.

I bought the ring at the beginning of October. I hadn't told anyone I had purchased it and decided the first person I had to tell was Alex, who was 8 years old at the time.

Telling an 8-year-old he had to keep such a big secret for 6 weeks was tough, and to Alex's credit, he kept the secret the entire time. Scott was next, along with Jim the plumber. He was the best plumber.

When my father-in-law visited, he gave me his blessing, with a hug, and called me "Son" for the first time. I grew up without a father-figure, and to hear it for what felt like the first time ever in my life was very foreign. I waited till our wedding day to call Mr. Bob Brinker "Dad" because I am superstitious, but I have called him Dad ever since.

My mother-in-law came up just as promised a couple weeks later for Angela's birthday. They went shopping for the day, and I spent the afternoon with Alex, who I wouldn't see all weekend, and I let him know, that starting tomorrow morning, he could tell anyone he wanted that I was going to propose. I remember his reaction of relief that he wasn't going to mess up the surprise, it was almost over.

When the ladies came back from shopping and started getting ready for dinner, Angela was upstairs, and my mother-in-law was curling her hair in our downstairs dining room mirror. I brought the ring out and showed her and asked if I could marry her daughter. I remember her covering her mouth and tears welling up and hugging me. I told her that I would be proposing over the weekend when I surprised Angela at dinner with a trip to Vegas.

Dinner that night, I handed Angela the itinerary for Vegas, which we were leaving for at 6am the next morning. My wife was thrilled with a sudden trip. All was set, all she had to do was pack for the weekend. Alex went back to his mother's house after dinner, and the packing began.

Reasons why I don't plan trips? I am terrible at preparing for delays. In theory, we should be able to make the show after we get off the plane, assuming everything is on time. It never is. Our first flight out of Kalamazoo had a mechanical problem, and we were told it wouldn't be fixed till lunchtime. We went to get breakfast and came back, and the flight had already left, just 45 minutes after it was originally supposed to leave. We wound up catching a later flight, that would still allow us to meet our layover in Chicago. When there is nothing to do in an airport though, a lot of times you find yourself at the bar, and my wife did just that. After about 3 drinks, she looked at me, and said,

"Are you going to propose?"

Angela had never asked me this question ever. Drunk Angela was making jokes and being funny and asked. She laughed to herself, and almost as if she had forgotten what she asked, changed the subject to what Casinos we were going to go to. We made it into Vegas 20 minutes before our show was starting and decided to skip it. To this day, we have never seen "The Blue Man Group."

Visiting the places that the clickbait link said were great to propose at, there is something very accurate in the slogan, "The City that Never Sleeps." The Gondola ride has lines to get on it, and there is a guy driving the boat. The top of the Eiffel tower at 2am had a line of people trying to get on it. Anywhere you looked, at any time of the day, it was busy. There is no down time. I wanted to be personal with my proposal and make it about us, not having a show, which would be very predictable of me, because I do love an audience in most things I do. I carried this ring with me in my pocket all day, looking for the right place and feeling to ask. In public in Vegas, there is no such thing as private.

Saturday evening, before we went to see "Cirque Du Soleil" while in our hotel room, and Angela searching through the hotel amenities book, I got down on one knee, reached my hands out with the little box, opened it and said,

"I love you; will you marry me?"

Angela paused, looking up from her research with wide eyes and said,

"What?"

I should have considered this a moment of shock, here I was nervous, even after 7 years, to ask this wonderful woman to be my wife, a title really because we were together, but I was rather disappointed I didn't plan better. In a hotel room, in Las Vegas, I asked the most important question of my life. I sat up and started explaining this, not really understanding that she hadn't said "yes" yet, and Angela just sitting in silence, finally breaking it with,

"Is this real? Are you serious?"

I snapped out of it, laid against the headboard on the bed, and embarrassed just thinking about, almost pouting, because everything I envisioned with asking her didn't work. I began to tell her how I came about proposing, and like my wife always does, she re-focused on the importance of the moment, interrupting me with,

"Yes."

Yes, she would marry me. Yes, we were going to get married.

Yes.

She put on her ring, called her sister and her mother. Took pictures, but neither of us were big on social media at the time, so it was just us. The personal moment I had strived to create in this overwhelming city was not wasted on a casino hotel room. It didn't matter where it was, or how it was done, the two of us were together, alone, and I wouldn't have it any other way.

We have told this story of our engagement and trip to Las Vegas many times over the years, and Rowan remembered often that the buffets were one of my favorite attractions. If there is one thing that Vegas does right, better than anyone else, it is buffets. I hadn't eaten much over the course of the trip because I was so nervous, but now that we were engaged, I started to feel like myself again, and that person was hungry. I could rank the buffets in Las Vegas based on the 6 I would visit over the next 2 days, but they are all world class food with a casual feel. The buffet at the LUXOR was my favorite overall with super fancy mixed drinks, desserts, Wolfgang Puck pizza, and filet mignon the size of your head. It's a weird segue from our engagement story to the quality of buffets, but my wife knew what she was marrying, and I think she is happy.

## What a Joker is used for

*"Day 71...*

*While grocery shopping with my wife she was insistent that we buy healthy and only healthy things... but made me in charge of the cart... and left me to my own devices...*

*So... Kraft makes the best mac n cheese, M&M's have cheesecake flavors now, Mountain Dew has watermelon flavor, Coke makes coffee, Doritos come in a 3-D version, Smart Food popcorn has snickerdoodle flavor, and Cinnamon Toast Crunch makes their own milk... I didn't get down the Oreo aisle...*

*My 8-year-old can bite his toenails and I am not sure if I am impressed or disgusted... I think a little of both...*

*February is pancake month... that's 28 days of pancakes... that's my 8-year-olds favorite food... he got ripped-off of 3 days having February as the month..."*

*"Day 72...*

*I once ate a fruit salad doused in vodka served in a giant watermelon... I have never eaten watermelon again... I tell you this, because the story escaped my memory until I took a drink of Watermelon Mountain Dew... it's not for me...*

*I forgot I bought cookie dunks for my 8-year-old... he found them and exclaimed my continued dominance as the World's Greatest Father...*

*He did say that the Cinnamon Toast Crunch milk was gross...*

*I know this is a tough title to hold, but I believe my son holds the title for the most lost gloves and winter hats in a school year… it is a pandemic year, so the playing field is not as full…*

*My wife is annoyed that the 3-D Doritos don't just admit that they are Bugles…*

*I couldn't play video games today… not because I had something to do, but because I don't have curtains for my windows in my basement and the snowy ground forced a blinding shield on the screen…*

*I guess I could hang blankets up like I did in college…"*

*"Day 73…*

*After doing the calculations of what I would have made if Day Trader apps allowed me to buy GameStop stock, I could have paid off my house… let's hope they let me buy Blockbuster when Reddit says its time…*

*Rowan overheard me say the "F" word today while I was on the phone, which I am not known to do in front of him… He didn't say anything until I was done with my phone call and then told me he couldn't wait to tell his mother on me… I said, "Huh, I'm an adult, I can say that if I want to, your mother can't stop me."*

*I'm a little worried about being told on…*

*My wife is a "half-eater" … Our friend dropped off carrot cake sandwich cookies… there is one that is half eaten and put back in the package… what a quitter… they never win…*

*Rowan was cleaning the basement and found a joker from a deck of cards... he asked me what to do with it... I said to throw it away... now I have to wonder what games the joker is ever used for... I'll google it later..."*

*"Day 74...*

*Our friends came over last night for the first time since the summer and we stayed up way later than people with children should do... if the clock says 2:30am, and you have an 8-year-old, that beats the hell out of having to get up for work or school in the morning...*

*On the bright side, "Jack in the Box" games has a 7th addition...*

*Rowan was playing "Madden Football" today and again, I really enjoy hearing his trash talk... instead of saying,*

*"I'll see you in Hell", he says,*

*"I'll see you in Heaven."*

*It doesn't sound as tough, but I love his confidence...*

*After eating these carrot cake sandwich cookies, I understand why Trader Joe's has a line to get in...*

*"The Best of the Best" was on today... a few things here... James Earl Jones plays the head coach of the USA National Karate team... Eric Roberts and Christopher Penn are on this team... this movie is a "B" version of "Roadhouse" meets Jean Claude Van Dam's entire film catalogue...*

*I watched this alone, because if my wife sees it, I am sure she won't sit through better action movies like "Young Guns" or "The Running Man", which she has never seen...*

*I have questionable taste in entertainment..."*

*"Day 75...*

*My across-the-street neighbor was shoveling his drive, so I texted him, "Missed a spot."*

*If this was done to me, I would not have laughed, but Dad Jokes are kind of my thing... he was nice enough to text back "LOL" ...*

*A big part of growing up is recognizing exactly when" Mounds" and "Almond Joy" candy bars sound good... as a kid, I would throw those out at Halloween...*

*We got a new kitten, and we have yet to name it, but Rowan suggested "Ash" and immediately I broke out the puns...*

*"Stop being an Ash-hole"*

*"You're a pain in my Ash"*

*And the recently remembered favorite,*

*"Back that Ash Up" ....*

*Rowan found these hilarious... but my wife is an adult...*

*Still no name for the kitten..."*

Googling,

"What is the joker card used for?",

this is the answer that pops up first from Wikipedia:

"The Joker's use varies greatly. Many card games omit the card entirely; as a result, Jokers are sometimes used as informal replacements for lost or damaged cards in a deck by simply noting the lost card's rank and suit on the Joker"

This answer bothered me enough to then ask,

"What card games use Jokers?"

The first answer is, "Euchre".

If you are from the Midwest, you know what Euchre is, although I would argue, Euchre is strictly a Michigan game, and we don't use Jokers. However, the answer on Britannica.com says,

"The joker was originally invented (though not under that name) to serve as the highest trump in the game of Euchre and is, in effect, a glorified Jack."

There is then a list of games that use the Joker in them, with all different uses. It is now my goal to play a game that uses the Joker in it, and it will not be Euchre.

Not too long after Raven's (our kitten) passing, we decided that Cecelia needed a playmate. Her whole life was surrounded by another cat to snuggle with and run her ragged throughout the day. She was lost as it was, and Bob the cat wasn't coming around to it. While buying cat food one day at the pet store, they had a Calico kitten who had just gotten through a deadly illness that only 5% survive.

She was cuddling another kitten, or trying to, and was low in weight, but she was on the mend. Rowan approached the cage, and she showed signs of interest. He hadn't been spending much time with Cecelia because of the pain of loss from Raven, but he smiled with this little Calico. Angela and I decided we would put an application in for adoption.

The Calico cat came home, and we began to juggle names. After a few weeks of brainstorming, we settled on Tori. Tori never sleeps, sometimes cuddles, but does things in pattern. For instance, she will lay on my chest in bed, and allow me to pet her while I watch TV, but I cannot pet her anywhere else in the house, just in bed, watching TV. She will allow my wife to hug her and put her on her shoulder, but only while my wife is standing on the side of our bed next to the on-suite bathroom. She doesn't handle disruption of these moments well, but at least she isn't destructive. If it sounds familiar, then you are thinking of Riley the blind chihuahua.

Rowan still holds her at a distance, and although I believe he loves his 3 cats, he doesn't have the bond he did with Raven. Life lessons are tough, but I would argue that parents watching their children learn the hard lessons of life are some of the most devastating moments of parenthood.

## The Trophy Husband

*"Day 76...*

*I have two pairs of Adidas Samba Classics... one is for yard/construction/bar work, and the other are my fancy shoes... I am having a hard time deciphering them now and need to probably buy another pair...*

*When you buy Little Caesar's for your son because you can't muster the energy to cook, it's the worst when the pizza has obviously been sitting... bright spot... I don't want any...*

*The highlight of the day was toilet shopping and now I absolutely want a bidet...*

*I haven't had a cookie since Friday... today is Monday... that's coming close to a record...*

*While my wife does Bible study with my 8-year-old I am going to exercise...*

*Whatever it takes..."*

*"Day 77...*

*I spent today remodeling our on-suite bathroom and when it was time to put the new vanity in, it had a stress fracture in the frame... special order... 2 weeks out for a replacement... and I had the old sink and vanity ripped out... who needs to wash their hands?...*

*Whoever invented a diet where you can only consume bacon and lose a ton of weight is brilliant... Who needs arteries?*

*"Styx" is an underrated super band and "A Star is Born" (Lady Gaga version) is an underrated movie...*

*When Rowan goes to bed at night, I say, "You know the deal", which means, "I love you very much." He said it last night before I left the room for the first time...*

*That is what is going to get me through the day..."*

*"Day 78...*

*The second time I can say, the LAST DAY!*

*My 8-year-olds task job at school is to water plants... my wife is a Master Gardener... I haven't watered a plant in 20 years...*

*The blind chihuahua barks for her dinner until we serve it... she eats at 5... she's been barking since 4... she's the worst...*

*My eldest son uses Door Dash daily, and twice this week from Tim Horton's... they gave him extra donuts and he feels they are flirting with him... I like the confidence... They can flirt with anyone, and they chose him... the donut shop... that's my boy!*

*Rowan asked Alexa who won the Super Bowl in 2017... she offered to tell him a story... so he accepted... the story wasn't all that great apparently, because Alexa asked him if it was as good story? He paused, contemplating whether it would hurt her feelings, and said, "No, it just wasn't for me, that's all."*

*He will be taking all telemarketer calls that come to my phone from now on...*

*I've been cleared to re-open by the Health Department, this is it again...*

*Weird coincidence, today is February 3rd... the Anniversary of my first date with my wife..."*

My wife and I married in the month of April. A little over 9 years past our first date. She left for a hotel the night before with her mother and sister, after we practiced for hours at the lower level in the pub for our first dance. I stayed home with Alex and played video games. My last night as an unmarried man. Before she left that night, I kissed her and whispered,

"Please don't forget to bring my wedding band.",

Joking, because it is the little things that Angela sometimes does that make our memories that much more vivid.

It was mid-afternoon and the church was full of family and friends. Scott was my best man, followed by my brother, and my 3 future brothers-in-law. My father-in-law walked my wife down the aisle, kissed her on the cheek, and offered her hand to me. She was beautiful and I felt undeserving, Angela has that effect on me. We were offered to do our vows, and we did, as it was time to place each other's rings on our fingers, Angela looked to me and whispered,

"Ok, don't freak out, but I forgot your ring in the back, and you will have to use Melissa's (Angela's best friend) ring."

There is a picture of this moment, that the crowd isn't quite sure of my reaction, and yet, it was probably our most favorite moment of what I consider a surreal day. There was dancing, and great food, and speeches, and happy reunions of people that hadn't seen each other in some time, but it all passes by so fast that when people ask you about it, you're never quite sure how to answer what you remember most. I do remember how my wife looked, how she felt to my touch. How happy this day was.

Someday, if I can make it to my senior citizen years, and retire, I hope that I can look back at my life and be proud of what I have accomplished and continue to be happy with who I spent it with. I hope both of my sons are more successful and fulfilled with their life choices than I am, which will be hard, because I have it good. I hope to see grandchildren that are close to me, and I might even inherit the name for "Papou" which is Greek for grandpa. I hope my wife still loves me when I am old and grey, and that we can look back on all of our life and think, "We did the damn thing."

Life isn't always about being happy or succeeding. My failures and regrets have shaped me more than I ever thought they would. I hope I keep evolving and become a better version of myself each day.

I often joke to my wife, that I am a trophy husband, with sarcasm in my voice. I refer to lazy nap days, and sugar binges in sweatpants and the avoiding of physical fitness as attributes of greatness in an ironic way.

I never had a plan of marriage, or a person who I could absolutely say,

"You are my one".

It was given to me, or discovered between us as a couple, or something else. I may never know why we work the way we do. I don't know if it was God's plan, or what that plan is for the future, but I am hopeful, and happy to know, it will be Angela and I, meeting all that comes before us.

Isn't that all you can hope for?

*Day 79.... And counting....*

## ABOUT THE AUTHOR...

Ted Vadella is the co-owner of Shakespeare's Pub in downtown Kalamazoo, MI. He is the creator of Dad Joke Genius and a co-creator of the Universal Snack Patrol. He resides with his wife, Angela in Portage, MI.

*The strongest person I have ever known… I was raised safe, and happy, and I have lived a life fulfilled. My mother means more to me than I could ever say…*

*From funny, pics, St. Patrick's Day costumes, a cheesy smile, and a brain freeze…*

# *Rowan*

*A rare photo of my adult, eldest son, Alex. How far we have come... You will always be my buddy...*

*"Go back in time" ....*

*Don't let the photo fool you... This dog was the worst... I miss her more than she deserves... Rest in Peace, my beautiful tulip... I am sure God has made room between his legs for you to sleep...*

*The infamous undercut! If you're not laughing, you're crying... It does look like SpongeBob's house though...*

*The fixed product. Considering what he had to work with, I would say that Colby is one heck of a hair stylist….*

*I am not good at taking pictures,*
*and all she wants me to do is smile.*

***So she tried singing.... it sort of worked...***

Made in the USA
Columbia, SC
23 January 2023

10119765R00172